You Talk Too Much

You Talk Too Much

A Wife's Guide to Becoming a Silent Warrior

Tanya DeFreitas
Love Wins Publishing
Redlands, California
2018

Copyright © 2018 by LaTanya DeFreitas

Love Wins Publishing
Redlands, California

Cover Design: Ace Pub
Editor: Dr. O.J. Mack

All rights reserved. This book or any portion thereof may not be reproduced or used in any manner whatsoever without the express written permission of the publisher except for the use of brief quotations in a book review.

Scripture quotations are from the New International Version, the King James Version, the New King James Version, and/or the English Standard Version of the Holy Bible. Definitions are from Merriam-Webster.com

Printed in the United States of America

First Printing, 2018

Dedication

This book is dedicated to every person who positively sowed into my marriage. Your words of encouragement, instruction, and wisdom have strengthened me and helped mold me into a silent warrior. May you be blessed with a double portion for being a blessing to me. ♥

Contents

Foreword 9

Introduction 11

Chapter 1: **Shut Your Mouth** 15

Chapter 2: **Pause and Pray** 27

Chapter 3: **Your Role: A Suitable Helper** 37

Chapter 4: **Your Assignment: Pray** 49

Chapter 5: **Respect: A Mandate** 59

Chapter 6: **Sex & Intimacy** 73

Chapter 7: **Be Intentional** 83

Chapter 8: **Silent Warrior** 93

Chapter 9: **The Power of Love** 103

Chapter 10: **The Power of Confessions** 111

The Task 117

Resources and Recommendations 119

Confessions of Faith 121

The Scripture Says 135

Other Books by the Author 139

Book Recommendations 141

Book Club Discussion Starters 145

First Comes Love Marriage Retreat 147

Wife Talk 148

Resources for Domestic Violence 150

Acknowledgements 151

Foreword

Beloved,

    If you are married or thinking about getting married, this book will revolutionize your way of thinking about communication! Here, you will learn about applying biblical principles to ensure what you say is in alignment with God's ultimate love language and way to communicate; prayer. This book is not just easy to read and implement, but has been written and inspired by Tanya DeFreitas, after spending time in prayer.

    In this book, you will find real-life experiences and practical knowledge, which has been applied by the author and has actually worked in her marriage. Each page of the book will provide you with Godly counsel. You will be encouraged by Tanya's level of transparency, her courage, and encouragement to you, as a wife.

    My name is Kristina Coleman. I am an inspirational speaker, bestselling author, educator, and an ordained minister. My life passion is to help others walk fully into their purpose. I have three beautiful children: Kiersten, Kristopher, and Kaleb. I have been married to my wonderful husband, Eddie, for more than 18 years.

As a seasoned wife, I assure you that the book you are holding will bring hope to your marriage. You will develop an understanding of the importance of ensuring God and prayer are the focal points of your marriage. This book will provide you with resources to understand how to fight silently and become the woman of God and help-meet God has called you to be.

This book will change the way you view your spouse and the words you allow to come out of your mouth. It will provide you with the tools to pause, to ensure you are using your tongue and mouth to speak "life," instead of "death," into your spouse and marital relationship.

Your prayer life is about to change! This will impact your communication with your spouse and ultimately transform your marriage. Glory!

So, jump into this journey of transformation. If you learn how to properly communicate with your Heavenly Father through prayer, He will give you the wisdom on how to communicate with your spouse and strengthen your relationship. Your life will never be the same. Are you ready?

Let's begin!

In Him,

Mrs. Kristina Coleman

Introduction

"He who has ears to hear, let him hear." Matthew 11:15

Dear wives and wives-to-be,

Can I just be real with you? I am not here to tell you what to do or how to do it. I am not here to be grammatically correct or proper. I am not a Bible scholar and I am not a relationship expert.

Everything I am getting ready to share is from my personal experience and journey. You can take it or leave it. You may agree or disagree. I am simply sharing what worked and is working for me and others I know. My hope is that it will work for you, as well.

Some of what I share will apply to you and some of it will not. Take what you need and save the rest for another time or another wife. If you are a single woman who desires marriage, please be advised that the Bible says, in marriage there will be trouble. Pay close attention to the content of this book. It will help you avoid not all, but some challenges that may arise.

I often hear others say, "Communication is key" in marriage. In this case, *key* means crucial, significant or important. Communication is an exchange of information. It is also the successful conveying or sharing of ideas and feelings. Communication in marriage matters, however the real key in marriage is prayer.

Prayer is communicating with God, the Creator. Prayer is crucial and very important in any relationship, especially marriage. In fact, prayer should be a foundation and a covering for marriage. I am not talking about praying out load for show or so that others can hear you. I am talking about going into your secret place, going into your prayer closet, getting on your knees or your face, and getting personal and real with God.

I have found that too often we go to others more than we go to God concerning our marriage. We use the excuse of needing to vent or wanting to get something off of our chest. We get in our feelings and we tend to make decisions that ultimately hurt our marriage.

Feelings are fickle. Feelings are inconstant, flighty, and unfaithful. To take how you feel, craft it into words, then speak it, can be dangerous.

In the heat of an argument, with your husband, you may feel like you do not want to be married anymore. You are in the middle of an argument; your feelings in that moment seem very real. You probably feel hurt, afraid, angry and all sorts of emotions. The next day, however, after you and your husband may have made up, you no longer feel hurt, afraid, or angry. In this moment, you want your marriage.

During the argument, you may have used words that you meant because of your emotional state. In your feelings, you pick up the telephone and call your girlfriend and tell her how you feel. You speak with your mouth that you do not want your marriage and you do not care if your husband leaves. You talk too much! You just planted seeds and those seeds will take root and manifest, if you are not careful.

How does talking to your girlfriends help your marriage? How does venting to someone else about your husband help him? It may help you temporarily because you no longer feel the need to vent or the desire to get something off of your chest. But how does talking to your girlfriends really help your marriage and your husband?

Women have a knack for communication. We like to talk. We like to talk with our friends. We like to share how we feel and we encourage one another to share what we think. In reality, we talk too much and often forget the power of our words.

The truth is we should not be talking to our girlfriends about our marriage and our husbands unless we are speaking words that encourage and edify. Our girlfriends should not know all of our frustrations, issues, and concerns regarding our husbands. We should not disclose his shortcomings and his inadequacies with anyone other than God.

God created marriage. It is His design and His institution. Who else knows how to help you navigate your marriage other than the One who created it? Who else knows any better how to deal with your husband than the One who created him?

My sister, do you know the power you possess as a wife? Do you understand that you can go directly to God? You do not have to tell your girlfriends or even your husband every feeling you have. Did you know that when you go to God, He will lead you, guide you, give you words to speak, and tell you when to keep quiet? God, not your girlfriends, has the power to touch your husband's heart and turn a situation around.

It took some time for me to truly grasp the power of my influence as a wife and the power of my words within my marriage. I spoke words and planted seeds of doubt, bitterness, and unforgiveness. I spread the seeds to my friends and to my family. Soon, they too were speaking words and planting seeds of doubt, bitterness, and unforgiveness into MY marriage.

For the sake of this book, communication is not key in marriage. <u>Communication is important; however the key to a healthy marriage relationship is prayer.</u> Mastering the art of silence and becoming a silent warrior is a golden key to the success of your marriage. I am going to show you how I used this key to turn my marriage around for the better.

Xoxo♥,

Mrs. Tanya DeFreitas

Chapter 1

Shut Your Mouth

"When words are many, transgression is not lacking."
Proverbs 10:19

"Just shut up!" he said.

And I did. I did not shut up because he told me to. I shut up because I was shocked. This was not the first time he said this to me, but this time was different.

"You talk too much!" he continued.

My heart traveled to my throat, creating a lump-like feeling. My lips and tongue were paralyzed. I was unable to say anything. In the past, I had my comeback ready. My tongue was slick and sharp, but this time I was rendered speechless.

All of my life I enjoyed talking. I was good at it. In grade school, I enjoyed giving speeches and standing in front of the class to talk. I had many friends because I showed myself friendly. I talked to other kids, easily. I really enjoyed talking.

In college, I spoke on behalf of the entire student population as their elected student body President. In fact, I spoke in different classes and events while I campaigned to be elected. During this period of my life, my grandmother told me I should study politics and run for a government position because I talked a lot and I was good at it.

In church, I served as Assistant to Pastor, at different ministries. I read the morning church announcements to the congregation and I was the mistress of ceremony at major church events. If there was an open microphone opportunity for testimonies, I was first in line. Talking was my thing and I took delight in it.

I was fond of talking so much that I majored in Communication in undergraduate school. Yes, I took classes in and studied everything I could about communication. After graduating college, I served as a Public Relations Assistant and an Advertising Sales Coordinator. Both positions involved lots and lots of people interface and talking.

In my mind, I was a great communicator and no one could tell me any different. Yet, for the first time in my adult life, as a married mother, I was told that I talk too much. And I have to admit, it was true.

OUR STORY

My husband, Rafael, and I met in Florida. I was training there for a new job back in California, which is where I am originally from. Florida was my home for almost three months. I was excited about meeting new people, making friends, and exploring my temporary home. I was not looking for a relationship, a hookup, or anything of that nature. In fact, I was already in a relationship when I met my husband. It was a dull and dead relationship, but nevertheless I was seeing someone.

Rafael and I met online. After messaging back and forth for several days, we exchanged telephone numbers. Our communication continued using text messaging. Then, we finally had our first telephone conversation.

We talked for a couple of hours. This was right up my alley. He happened to be a good listener and he was quite engaging. I learned that he was a writer, like me, and he was a communicator, like me. He was not looking for a relationship, a hookup, or anything of that nature either and he understood my visiting circumstances. Jackpot!

We decided to meet in person. He was going to be the new friend to give me a tour of Florida. We both enjoy the ocean so our first meeting was at the beach.

After the face to face introduction, we enjoyed the warm sun, the gentle breeze, and the beautiful blue water, with our feet in the sand. We talked and talked, for hours. We met at 5 p.m. on a Friday and we talked until 7 a.m. Saturday morning.

Yes, we talked for 14 hours! I am not exaggerating! There was no hanky panky, we did not even kiss, and we remained in public the entire time. The conversation was so good neither of us wanted it to end and we honestly lost track of time.

We were so intrigued by one another, both wanting to understand God's purpose for our meeting. After a moment of what seemed like the first silence in hours, Rafael asked me if we could pray together. I think that is the moment I fell in love!

After an amazing week with Rafael, I flew back to California to spend time with my children for the weekend before returning to work. Leaving Florida for just a few days seemed like the hardest thing to do. I was excited to see my children; however, I did not want to leave Rafael. It felt like I was leaving a part of me behind. It was the worst and best feeling I had experienced. When I arrived to California, the first thing I did was end the dull and dead relationship. I had met someone new and he had given me a new hope.

I enjoyed a fabulous weekend with my children before going back to work in Florida. Again, it was a bittersweet feeling as I left my children, and was returning to Rafael. We had planned to meet for dinner upon my return. I was going to pick up the rental car, go to my hotel, shower, and then change before meeting him for dinner.

When my plane landed in Florida, after texting my mother and children, I texted Rafael to let him know I had arrived. To my surprise, he was already at the airport waiting for me. This was the beginning of his sweet gestures and surprises for me.

Rafael and I had an amazing connection. Things were going really well, but the reality was I lived in California and he lived in Florida. I remember silently praying and asking God why this man had come into my life. He had so many qualities that I desired in a mate, but he was in Florida so it made no sense to me.

During my silent prayer, I asked God to give me a sign to confirm if Rafael was the man to love me. I prayed silently on purpose. I did not want the enemy to hear my prayer so that when my answer came I would know it was from God. I specifically asked God for a gesture. I needed God to prompt Rafael to do something that would move me, but only God knew it would move me.

The following day, during his lunch break, Rafael asked me to meet him in the parking lot of his apartment complex. I pulled up next to his work truck and he came over to open my door (like he always does). I turned to grab my purse, thinking

I was getting out of the car, and when I turned back towards him, he had a bouquet of roses for me.

This may seem minor; however, it was the gesture I prayed for. No one knew I prayed for this besides God. One reason I prayed for this gesture was because it was something that I desired, yet lacked in my previous relationships. In that moment, I knew. I never knew anything like I knew right then.

<u>Within three weeks of meeting, Rafael proposed and I said, "Yes!"</u> Yep, we were engaged within three weeks. From the first date on, we spent every day together, except when I flew home to see my children.

Prior to the engagement, we fasted together in an effort to get God's approval for our relationship. Rafael also took me to meet his mother, one of his brothers, one of his sisters, his daughter, his ex-wife, and a few of his friends. Again, things were going really well. We talked a lot, laughed a lot, drove around town so that I could sightsee, and we prayed together regularly.

My time in Florida eventually came to an end. It was time for me to fly back home to California. We were going to try to maintain a long distance relationship and figure things out over time. I would visit him and he would visit me, we would video chat, and talk over the telephone, regularly.

Two months after I left Florida, however, Rafael resigned from his job as a Cable Technician, packed up, and relocated to California. Within the first few days of being in California, he asked my grandfather and my mother for my hand in marriage. Four months later we were married.

TROUBLE IN PARADISE

In the beginning of a relationship, communicating is vital. It is one of the ways that we get to know the other person. In the beginning of a relationship, we are also very kind, extremely considerate, and putting our best foot forward.

Remember when you first met your husband? Were you attentive, interested, and just as sweet as pie? I know I was. I wanted to know everything about him. I listened. I was understanding and supportive. I did not interrupt him when he spoke. Even if I disagreed with him I did not make a big deal. Oh how things changed after getting married.

Our first argument was about sex. Yes, ma'am. He had his preferences and I had mine. Both of us had experiences prior to one another so we also had a set of expectations that we entered the marriage with. We thought we talked about everything before getting married, but if there is one thing marriage is good for it is bringing out all of the mess we have inside of us.

Shortly after the sex argument was a disagreement about finances. Then, there were arguments about cooking, cleaning, parenting, friendships, Facebook, and more. It started to seem like we were arguing about everything. We were experiencing a breakdown in communication.

Of course, I was not the problem. I was the one with a degree in Communication so there was no way I was the problem. He had the problem and I needed to help him fix his problem so we could live happily ever after.

Yea, ok.

TALKING TOO MUCH

As the problems and arguments between my husband and I increased, I would vent to my mother, his mother, my sisters and girlfriends. I did not think I was doing anything wrong. I was just venting and getting things off of my chest.

I would tell my mother how frustrated I was with my husband and give her examples. In the beginning of me inviting her into my marriage, she would respond positively trying to encourage me and speaking highly of her new son-in-law. I continued to share the bad and the ugly about him to the point that it wore on her. I painted an ugly picture of my husband. As far as I was concerned, he was the most annoying person in my life and he did not know how to communicate.

When I called his mother to tell her about her son I came from a different angle. I still vented my frustrations. I still pointed the finger at him. I still told the bad and the ugly. I still painted an ugly picture of my husband.

His mother never joined in on seeing the ugly picture, however. Well, he is *her* son. No matter what I told her, she always advised me to pray. She always fed me the Word. She encouraged me and taught me how to fight in silence, but not before I vented to my girlfriends.

My girlfriends know me in a way that my mother does not know me. My girlfriends know intimate details of my past relationships and were able to help me compare my marriage to my past. They know my story and all that I have been through so they easily understood my frustrations during my vent sessions. My girlfriends were good at letting me get it all out and helping me stir the pot more. There was a time period when they too tried to defend my husband, but I made sure they knew enough about him to ensure that they could see the picture I painted.

I painted a very ugly picture of my husband. Every little wrong, every little fault, everything that annoyed me, I vented about. My words were like venom and I was poisoning my own life and my marriage. Despite his good qualities, I made my husband out to be an ugly, annoying person.

The truth is I was annoying, as well. I was also being very ugly towards the person I should have been trying to learn and understand. The words I was speaking to others were creating the atmosphere in my home and setting the tone in my marriage.

I used to think my husband was clingy, when all he wanted to do was spend quality time with me. Remember, he relocated from Florida to California so he did not know anyone other than me (and my family) for a long time. I used to say I wish he had friends and would go hang with them and just leave me alone. Well, once he made friends and started hanging out, guess who had a problem with it? How dare he leave me home alone on a Friday night? The seeds I had sown with my words were manifesting and I did not like it.

THE BEGINNING OF THE END

There were things I did not like about my husband. There were things that I did not understand about him. I learned things about him, after we were married, that I did not know before we were married.

The things I did not like, I spoke on, every chance I got. My husband received more than a piece of my mind on several occasions. I over talked him. I interrupted when he was talking. I talked about him to others and sometimes I outright ignored him.

I was a strong woman who did not need a man. I was not going to let a man control me or tell me what to do. I had a voice and it would not be silenced. I was going to stand up for myself, speak up on my behalf, and fight, literally, if I had to. If he did not like it he could get on a plane and go back to where he came from. I did not give God any room to do anything because I did what I wanted to do and what felt good to my flesh. I was protecting myself. So I thought.

Nothing I was doing was working. He was not changing. He was not leaving. My marriage was not getting better.

I wore myself out trying to assert myself. I was completely disrespectful and out of order.

This cycle continued for a period of time. He would say something and I had something to say back. I continued to over talk him and interrupt him. We became truly frustrated with one another. There was bickering, stomping through the house, doors and cabinets slamming shut, sleeping on the edge of the bed, etc. That cycle got old. We were tired of it all. Our marriage was hanging on by a thread. Then, one day an argument ensued and as I opened my mouth to speak every evil word I could think of, he said, "Just shut up! You talk too much!"

He was right.

SHHHH! DO NOT SAY ANOTHER WORD

Wives, we have work to do. You and I were gifted to be in our role as a wife. God has an expectation of how we should utilize our gift(s). Many of us have been or still are caught up in thinking that we have to speak up for ourselves. We think we have to defend ourselves to our husbands and say whatever comes to mind. If you serve the same God that I serve, this way of thinking is not in line with the Word.

We have a responsibility in marriage. The Bible says that God is our vindicator. This holds true even with our husbands. You and I have an enemy. It is not our husbands. We are not fighting against flesh and blood. Our fight is spiritual and until we begin to fight using spiritual methods and tools we will not experience all of the blessings that are available.

Has it ever dawned on you that you may have everything it takes for your husband to be all he is supposed to be and that is why God allowed you to be his wife? I used to think I married the wrong person. When we started arguing and could not see eye to eye, I was convinced that I had messed up and missed the mark.

I was trying to right my wrong so I started praying my husband away. It may sound foolish or it may seem funny, but it is my truth. I started searching for sermons and videos on what to do when you marry the wrong person. Then, I learned that it is not about marrying the right person, it is about being the right person.

God has the power to transform any marriage and any person. I believe if God allows you to walk into a situation, He can help you get through it and conquer it. Even an unbelieving husband may start to believe when he has a wife who has mastered the art of silence and walking in God's love.

Ladies, shut your mouths! Shut your mouth to your girlfriends. Stop picking up the telephone to text or call anyone to complain or vent about your husband. When you do this, it is not helping your marriage, your husband or you and it is out of order.

If the state of your marriage involves a lot of arguing, tension, disagreements and the like; you probably talk too much. You probably respond when you should not. You probably say how you feel more than you should. You probably talk to one too many people about your marriage. Stop. Just stop. Shhhhhhhhhh! Don't say another word.

It is difficult to hear from God when there is noise and chaos clouding our minds and our lives. In order to hear from God, you have to shut your mouth, open your heart, and get quiet. When we become quiet we can hear on a different frequency. When we shut our mouths and tune in, we begin to hear what we need most.

Reflection

What are you saying about your marriage? What are you saying about your husband? Are you building your house? Or are you tearing it down, with your words?

Victory Verse

"Whoever keeps his mouth and his tongue keeps himself out of trouble." Proverbs 21:23

Prayer

Father God, in the name of Jesus, please forgive me for speaking harmful, hurtful, mean, and defensive words. Please forgive me for tearing others down with my mouth, especially my husband. Please forgive me for gossiping about my husband and our marriage. Set a guard over my mouth, O Lord and keep watch over the door of my lips. Let no corrupt talk come out of my mouth, but only such as is good for building up. Amen.

Confession

I open my lips to speak what is right. My mouth speaks what is true. My lips detest wickedness. All the words of my mouth are just; none of them are crooked and perverse.

Chapter 2

Pause and Pray

"Even fools are thought wise if they keep silent, and discerning if they hold their tongues." Proverbs 17:28

  The more you talk, the greater the chance of you sinning with your mouth. Have you noticed that when you are communicating with a girlfriend if you are not careful you can go from talking about yourself to talking about others? I have called my girlfriend to vent and I go from talking about why I am upset or bothered, to telling her what my husband did to upset or bother me.

  After we go back and forth on that topic for a little while, the conversation shifts. Before you know it we are talking about the next person's relationship or marriage and we are giving updates on family members or other friends. In essence, we are gossiping.

  Gossip is a casual or unconstrained conversation or reports about other people. Gossip is a sin. We have no business telling our girlfriends intimate details or gossiping about our husbands (or family members and other friends, for that matter).

PROTECT WHAT IS PRECIOUS

When you expose information about your husband you are betraying his confidence in you. You are positioning yourself to be an unsafe place for him. In Proverbs 31, the husband's heart safely trusts in his wife. In order for him to safely trust in her she has to be a safe place to go.

Safe places are safe! There is no judgment in a safe place. There are no threats, no discomfort, no discord, and no betrayal. A safe place protects. A safe place provides comfort and peace. Are you safe place for your husband? Can his heart safely trust in you?

We have to protect what is precious. In your marriage, your husband's heart and spiritual growth are valuable. You are not in this man's life to reveal to him all of his faults. You should not reveal his faults to your friends or other people either. The Bible says love covers a multitude of sin. Are you using love to cover your husband when you tell other people his shortcomings?

As a wife, you are going to learn things about your husband that his mother does not know. You are going to learn things that the children, his friends, his boss, his coworkers, and the Pastor do not know. It is not your place to tell anyone else what you learn about your husband.

If you have not already, you are going to learn things about your husband that you do not like. Protect what you learn about him. You have proprietary (or private) information about your husband on purpose. The purpose is not to expose him.

Protect the vulnerable things you find out about your husband. Protect his weaknesses. Protect his fears. Protect his shortcomings. Use your power of influence to create whatever he is lacking. Take what you discover or what is revealed to you about your husband to God in prayer. That is what you are supposed to do.

MARRIAGE IS SACRED

One reason we have so many marriages running amuck is because wives are doing way more talking than praying. You tell his business more than you ask God to help him and heal him. You call your girlfriends to tell them what is going on more than you get on your face and ask God how to deal with what is going on. We have to stop.

Ladies, I am not saying that talking with friends is wrong. Sure, you can talk with your friends. Sure, you can share things with them about how life is going as it relates to your marriage; however, there should be boundaries on what is disclosed. Marriage is sacred. What you and your husband go through behind closed doors is private and only to be shared if you both agree and share the details together.

Let me reiterate, marriage is SACRED! What you and your husband go through behind closed doors is private, with the exception of abuse. Abuse is not okay. Abuse must be exposed in order to be dealt with and for healing to take place.

Many women have walked away from abusive marriages and many women have stayed. I cannot make that choice for you. If you are in a situation where you are being physically harmed, however, for whatever reason, please confide in someone who has the ability to help you get to a safe place. In fact, if your life is in danger please seek the assistance of your local church, Pastor, a community organization, a friend, or family member, as soon as possible.

Please know that I am not advising any wife to divorce her husband. That is not my call, regardless of the circumstance or details. I am also not encouraging a wife to stay in an abusive situation. Sometimes, in cases where abuse is present, it is necessary to separate for safety and intervention.

As a believer of the Bible and God's Word, I know that God can turn the worst situation around and then allow it to be a testimony to someone else. I have witnessed restoration after infidelity. I have witnessed deliverance and healing after addiction. I have witnessed reconciliation after abuse.

God is Almighty and He can transform any marriage and any person. God honors marriage and the Bible says that God hates divorce (Malachi 2:16). In my opinion, this tells me that no matter what a marriage faces; God is able to turn things around. Marriage is sacred, just like God. If you or someone you know is experiencing spousal abuse, there is an information page with resources to help you, in the back of this book.

VENGEANCE BELONGS TO GOD

The Bible says that God is our vindicator. We have to allow God to be who He already is. I say, "allow" because the Bible tells us that God is our vindicator, however sometimes we seek vengeance on our own. When you make efforts to try to vindicate yourself, you hinder God's power to make moves on your behalf. No, we do not have the power to stop God. Absolutely not. Yet, when we take matters into our own hands, more often than not we mess things up and we get in the way of what God wants to do.

We are advised to be slow to speak. In fact, the scripture tells us to be quick to listen, slow to speak, and slow to become angry (James 1:19). When you feel the urge to call your girlfriend or whomever to vent, pause and pray. Take a few deep breaths, put your phone down, and go into prayer.

I know it is not easy. Sometimes we feel like we need to talk out what we are feeling or going through. Sometimes we want validation of our feelings or someone to tell us that we are not crazy for thinking or feeling a particular way. Sometimes we want to snap at our husbands because what he said or did really hurt.

God sees and knows your situation, at all times. Strive to get in a habit of going to your Maker. You can talk out what you are feeling with God. He will let you know if you are crazy or not. In fact, going to God is your best bet. Until you try it a few times, you will not know that what I am saying is true.

I remember my husband and I having a huge disagreement. He was at work and I was at home. He called me to tell me that he was upset. I listened. I did not speak a word. In fact, I began praying silently as he was talking.

As a result of my silence, my husband asked me if I had heard what he said. I answered, "Yes," and said nothing more. He was aggravated and hung up. Immediately, I went into prayer.

My feelings were hurt. I was on the verge of tears. He took something I did the wrong way and it hurt him. It was not my intent to hurt him; however, that is how he was affected.

I had my side of the argument, but I intentionally chose to not argue. Instead of telling my husband my side, I told God. God knew it was a misunderstanding. God knew I did not intend to hurt my husband. God also knew that I was trying to keep the peace, which is why I kept my mouth shut.

After praying, I did not feel better instantly. I was still hurt. I am human. I wanted to call my husband back and defend myself with my mouth, but I did not. I let it be. I knew God heard me and God would work it out somehow.

On this same day, about 2 hours after the phone call my husband came home during his lunch break. I had fallen asleep because when we get into heated disputes it drains me. After I pray sometimes I am physically exhausted so I lay down.

My husband came into our bedroom and woke me up. He asked me to come into our living room. Without a word and without hesitation, I got up out of the bed and followed him. Once we were in the living room, he turned to me, wrapped his arms around my waist, and he apologized. Hallelujah!

I did not have to argue my point. I did not have to give him a piece of my mind. I went to God and on my behalf God went to my husband. Ladies, God is Almighty! He has the power to get your husband to do what He wants him to do.

My husband told me that while he was driving in his work truck, God was dealing with him and told him to come home and apologize to me. God softened his heart to understand that it was not my intent to hurt him. My husband could have called me and apologized. He did not have to listen when God spoke to him, but he did listen. He was obedient. We squashed that matter and moved forward.

There was another time when my husband wanted to spend a significant amount of money on something I did not think any money should be spent on at all. I wanted to snap. I am just being honest. Instead of snapping, however, I held my tongue and prayed. He changed his mind about the purchase within minutes. All I could do was silently thank God.

THE ART OF SILENCE

There are countless times when I went to God with my frustrations, my fears, my concerns, my hurt, my disappointment, and he moved in my behalf, sometimes instantly. It did not start off this way because I did not start off doing things

God's way. I started off talking too much, but I learned to pause and pray.

Learning to be quiet, to pause and pray, does not come easy to someone who loves to talk. It is also not easy to some of us who have strong personalities, are natural leaders, and have a history of being independent. Learning to be quiet takes practice. The old saying is practice makes perfect.

When your husband approaches you operating under the influence of an argumentative spirit, pause and pray. When he comes at you in any way other than lovingly, pause and pray. You do not have to go into defense mode. Master the art of silence. Allow God to defend you. You do not have to respond, but if you do respond, do so in love. Be gentle and be kind.

The Bible says in Proverbs 15:1, "A soft answer turns away wrath." If your words are not soft, seasoned with love and encouragement, then do not say anything. You will get a better response from your husband if you are gentle and kind. You also give God room to do what He needs to do when you choose to not fight fire with fire.

We have to know when to let something go. If your husband is wrong, it will be revealed soon enough. It is much more powerful when God reveals it to him, than you revealing it to him. Sometimes you just have to say ok and allow the conversation or argument to settle. Make him hear more by saying less. Tell God and let God tell your husband.

As you begin to pause and pray with your husband, you will notice you will start to pause and pray in other areas of your life. The Bible says to pray without ceasing. How can we do that when we have jobs, class, grocery shopping, children, pets, etc.? You can pray silently and no one even knows you are praying besides you and God.

There was a time in my life when I thought I had to speak my prayers out loud. For whatever reason, my prayers felt more effective this way. As if God, the one who made me, could not hear my very thoughts, I used my mouth. You can pray in your mind and rest assured that God hears you (Mathew 9:4, Matthew 12:25, Mark 2:8, Luke 6:8, Luke 11:17).

Silence is golden. It really is. Try to think in a peaceful manner, try to speak in a peaceful manner, and try to act in a peaceful manner. Practice silence. As you do this and as you make an effort to pause and pray, you will begin to see things turn around in your marriage. This is the beginning process of becoming a silent warrior.

Stop arguing with your husband. Stop responding to things unnecessarily. Stop venting to your girlfriends. Watch your mouth and guard your lips. Be a wise woman.

Cultivate a meek and quiet spirit, which is precious to God (1 Peter 3:4). Learn the art of silence, pause and pray. You do not know what God is doing and wants to do with the man in your life. Take your mouth off of your husband and take your eyes off of him. Focus on God's Word and strive to be a peacemaker.

You have to learn when to be quiet and when to speak. It takes practice. It requires discipline and self-control. If you make an effort to hold your peace and trust God, He will speak to you in the midst of a situation to tell you if it is time to speak or be quiet. God will also allow things to happen to teach us, mold us, and shape us into a better being.

Like me, you may be a communicator. You may talk a lot on your job, at your church, or with your friends. In your marriage, it is different. We have to be in tune with the Holy Spirit so that we receive proper instruction on what to say, when to say it, and how to say it. Your role as a wife is an assignment. If you ask, God will show you how to deal with any given situation within your marriage. You have to become quiet to be led by God. Start today, pause and pray.

Reflection
Are you operating in self-control? Do you think before you speak? Are you a safe place for your husband?

Victory Verse
"Better to live on a corner of the roof than share a house with a quarrelsome wife." Proverbs 25:24

Prayer
Father God, in the name of Jesus, teaches me how to pause and pray. Help me to quiet my mind so that I can hear and be led by you in every situation in my life. Show when to speak and when to be quiet. Amen.

Confession
I am a peacemaker and I am blessed. The words of my mouth and the mediation of my heart are acceptable in God's sight. I rejoice in hope, I am patient in tribulation, and I am constant in prayer.

Chapter 3

Your Role: A Suitable Helper

"Then Lord God said, "It is not good for the man to be alone. I will make a helper suitable for him." Genesis 2:18

    Marriage is the highest form of relational commitment. It is recognized by God and the law. The law does not recognize boyfriend and girlfriend and neither does God or the Bible. This tells us how important the position of husband and wife and the roles in marriage are.

    After God created the earth, he created man and the animals. Then, He noticed something. There was no suitable helper for Adam.

    God recognized Adam's need for a helper and companion. It does not say that Adam asked for a helper. The need was identified by God. Not only was the need identified, but the method by which to meet the need was also identified.

    God caused Adam to fall into a deep sleep. He was made unaware as God prepared his suitable helper and companion. The Bible says that while Adam was unaware, in the deep sleep, God took one of his ribs.

He performed what we would today call a surgical operation. He opened Adam, took a rib, and closed Adam's body. From that one rib, as we know it, God formed and fashioned a woman. From that one piece of Adam's body God made another being. This being was presented to Adam, as his suitable helper, his companion. Her name was Eve.

THE PERFECT COMPLEMENT

In Hebrew, the name Eve means life. Eve is known as the mother of all the living. She is the first woman and the first wife. She did not have a natural mother or a natural father. She was not made from the dust of the ground like the first man. Eve was made by God, from the man creation. Eve was hand crafted and designed, especially for Adam.

In her original state, Eve was flawless. She was undefiled by any evil, unblemished by any disease or defect, unspoiled by any imperfection. Eve was created by God to be the pure and pristine ideal of womanhood.

Eve is the epitome of woman. She was not born into sin; she was royal, regal, and the living embodiment of humanity. She was designed from her husband and was the perfect complement for him. I imagine she personified the best trait of strength and beauty. Have you ever thought about what she may have looked like? The Bible does not mention her physical traits and that is the first point I want to make.

You were made in the image of God. You are needed and you are necessary. In Jeremiah 1:5, the Bible says that before God formed us, He knew us! He had us in mind! He created each one of us the way He wanted. We are designer brand, we are name brand! We are God's marvelous creation!

The Bible does not describe Eve's personal physical traits and probably on purpose. The Bible focuses on the biblical account of Eve's role and her assignment, alongside her husband. Her chief distinguishing traits of true feminine excellence are not superficial.

Ladies, no matter how pretty you are or how great your body is, what matters most are the traits that are unseen. Eve's body shape, size, hair color, hair length, etc. are not mentioned because they did not matter. What mattered was her role. What is your role?

You were created for purpose, just like Eve. You are necessary, just like Eve. Her outer appearance had no significance on her role, her duty, or her assignment. She had a role to play, a responsibility, and a purpose to fulfill, just like you and I.

Your focus should not be on your outward appearance. I am not saying do not take care of you. Get your hair done, get your nails done, and wear what makes you feel pretty, if that is your thing. I am saying what the Bible says in 1 Peter 3:3-4. Focus on your inner beauty, because therein lies your ability to operate in your role.

As a wife, you are the perfect complement to your husband. He needs you. He may not realize it, or maybe he does, but it is true. If your husband came already equipped with everything he needed and was already walking in his purpose, what would he need you for? If he did not need any help, why does he have a wife?

CALLED TO HELP

As a wife, you and I are called to help. Help is an action word. It requires doing. Help means to give assistance to or to come to the aid of. It also means to make it easier to do something. When you vent to your girlfriends or pop off at the mouth at your husband are you helping him?

Your husband was given authority over you, on purpose. This is a part of God's divine plan and order for the family. Your husband's authority includes watching over your well-being. Your role is to allow him to watch over you.

The position of wife should not be frowned upon or taken lightly. A wife is not a second class citizen. A wife is not less than her husband. You are necessary and God made that decision when He created a suitable helper for Adam. It is a blessing to be a wife when you embrace the gift in your role.

THE EXECUTIVE ASSISTANT

In the corporate world, most CEO's and upper level management have an Assistant. The Assistant is often assigned to one or several executives. The Assistant does a lot more than outsiders know and or see.

Assistants often hold down an entire office. They write letters and memos and the CEO signs them. They put together the material needed for the presentations that the CEO puts on. The Assistant holds a lot of power and strength. The Assistant is the right hand of the CEO and this is their role.

Most CEO's have a hard time functioning without an Assistant. They need an Assistant because they need help. Someone has to file, organize, oversee, and serve as a gatekeeper. The Assistant helps to make the CEO look great. The Assistant is a helper to the CEO.

As a wife, we are like Assistants, in fact, Executive Assistants, to our husbands. I do not mean that in a degrading manner at all. We serve God through serving as a helper to our husbands. Just like the CEO needs an Assistant, the husband needs a wife.

Like the Assistant, the wife holds a lot of power and strength. We organize, oversee, and serve as a gatekeeper of our homes. We set the tone of our homes. We have a direct connection with the Creator who is also the Founder and the President over our husbands.

Every successful CEO has someone they report to. Your husband, likened to CEO, is responsible to report to God. (If he is not reporting to God and being led by God in this moment, help him by doing your part and being an example before him). God is his covering. You on the other hand are responsible to your husband and your husband is your covering.

Adam was Eve's covering. Just like she had a role, so did he. A part of his role was to cover her. We do not know the details of why she was off by herself when the serpent came in to trick her. What we do know is that when Eve was away from her covering (her husband), and not focused on her role the enemy crept in and tricked her.

How many times have we been led astray or tricked because we stepped away from doing what we are supposed to do? What am I saying? When you step out of the divine order you leave room for the enemy to creep in and deceive you.

Learning to understand your role will help you to remain in order. Just knowing these things will not keep you in order, however. There is work required of you. There are things that you must do so that you stay in order and in right standing with God.

Instead of engaging the serpent, imagine if Eve had chosen to consult with her husband and did not give into the temptation? Had she been in line with her role as a suitable helper, remembering that she was accountable to her husband and they had been given an order by God, she may have been able to shut the enemy down and prevent her and her husband both from falling.

Assistants in the corporate world consult with the CEO about most major decisions. While the Assistant may be given authority to call shots and give orders, the Assistant is fully aware that every decision affects the CEO and the company. As an Assistant or help to your husband, yes you may have authority to do and act without consulting him. Keep in mind, however, that every decision you make, also affects your husband, just like Eve's decision.

DO NOT COMPLAIN

When I used my mouth to talk about my husband I was not helping him. In fact, I was hurting him and in turn hurting myself. As a married couple, God sees your husband and you as one. Yes, you are still an individual and so is your husband. Yes, you both are accountable to God individually; however, we cannot curse our husbands and think that we are not cursing ourselves.

I used to complain to God about my husband. Every little thing he did or did not do I pointed it out to God, as if God was unaware. I would pray that my husband would get in trouble with God to prove my own point(s). No matter how much I complained or how much I prayed for my husband to get in trouble with God, nothing changed. It seemed like God was more gracious and merciful to my husband when I complained or told on him.

Do you have a friend who complains or children who complain? Isn't it irritating being in the presence of someone who constantly complains? How do you think you sound going to God pointing the finger at your husband? I imagine it is not a sweet and pleasant experience for God to hear you and I pray against or complain about the person He has allowed to have authority over us.

It was not until my prayer changed that I started to see changes in my husband and my marriage. My prayer went from telling on my husband and pointing out his faults to asking God to help me in the midst of it all. I asked God for understanding and strength. I asked God to help me to do my part so that I could be pleasing to Him and hear clearly from Him.

The areas I was complaining about God showed me were areas I was supposed to help my husband in. My husband was quick tempered. I am the complete opposite, believe it or not. My husband does not trust others easily. I trust God so much that I rarely struggle with trusting others. My husband was reckless with finances. I am a budgeter. I am frugal and responsible with money. For every area he lacked, I had a level of strength in the same area and God began to show me how to help my husband in the areas I was complaining about.

Our role and duty is to help our husbands. When you are in the mind frame to help someone, you do not complain. When we give to the homeless or volunteer at the school or church, we do not complain. We are helping willingly.

Help your husband, willingly. Do not complain about who he is or what he is not doing. Help him become a better man. Help him step into his purpose. Help him develop and grow. We have to love the hell out of our husbands. Love them through their growth. Love them through their dark periods. Love them through their brokenness and filth. God loved you through yours.

HOW HELPING LEADS YOU TO PURPOSE

In helping and loving your husband, this does not mean it is okay to nag him or jump on his case about what he is not doing or where he may be lacking. This does not mean throw scripture at him when he falls short or remind him to get right with God. If he chooses not to go to church, ok. That is his choice. If he chooses to hold on to a bad habit, like smoking cigarettes, or cursing from time to time, ok. We cannot force these grown men to do anything and we should not even try.

You are not your husband's Pastor. Nagging him and reminding him of what he is not doing is not going to change him or your marriage. We are called to help, not lead. We are called to help, not take over. It is not our job to change our husbands. We can only change ourselves.

God created Eve for Adam. Eve was Adam's suitable helper. You are your husband's suitable helper. God chose you for your husband because you are strong enough to help him. There is something in you that your husband needs. Give it to him!

Being a helper does not mean you do not have a purpose that is apart from being a wife. There are gifts, talents, and abilities that God placed inside of you. You will utilize those gifts, talents, and abilities in various areas of life. We have to position ourselves to be in right standing so that everything we are supposed to have, do and be will flow and be in order.

I have often felt angry and frustrated as a wife; feeling like my husband is holding me back. There are certain things that my husband does not like or agree with. To me what he does not like or agree with translates into a delay in me using my God given gifts, talents, and abilities.

I am naturally ambitious and eager. I am a go-getter and a goal digger. Once I see my target in my mind, I run towards it without taking a breath. My husband, however, is not the same. My husband is more cautious. He has to think things through. He has to adjust to things that for me come natural.

I have had to learn to slow down. I have had to learn to sit on a thing before taking it on. I have had to learn that I do not need to reply to a text, instant message, or email right away. Breathe. Pause and Pray.

This has been a tough lesson for me. I am still learning how to slow down and how to sit on something before taking it on. The point I am trying to make here is the need for you and I to focus on our role and being in right standing with God. When we do this, God will work the rest out.

You will get to where you are supposed to go. Your husband cannot stop Gods plans for your life. No one can stop Gods plan for your life, not even you. You can slow down the process, but you cannot stop what God already said will be.

It may seem like your husband is getting in the way of you starting your business or building your ministry. What if God is using your husband to slow you down? What if there is something you still need to learn before you leap? Do no rush the process. Trust God, His way, and His timing.

Our job is not to micro manage our husbands or to dictate their process and journey. Our job is to pray! If your husband is out of position, pray him into position. Pray for his deliverance. Pray that heeds the leading of the Holy Spirit.

Listen, I am not trying to encourage wives to remain in a miserable situation. Sure, you can leave. You can file for divorce if you choose to. However, the very thing that God is trying to teach you through this relationship, you are going to have to learn one way or another.

God hates divorce! You entered a covenant with God and your husband. God takes covenant seriously and we should to! God hates divorce and he honors marriage.

Even if you chose your husband in your brokenness and now you have someone who you think is not ready to lead and is not worthy of your respect, he is still your husband. Your best bet is to pray like never before. It is a task and it will probably be challenging, but you made a commitment. Commitment is doing what you said you would do after the mood you said it in is gone.

God can and will transform marriage We are not supposed to keep tabs on what our husbands are or are not doing. If we focus on doing what we are supposed to do we should not have much time to focus on what our husbands are not doing. If we are not focusing on what our husbands are not doing it leaves very little room for the need to vent to surface.

Take a seat. Back off of your husband's back. Stop nagging that man! Shift your focus on you and doing your part. Work out your own salvation to fulfill your own purpose. In the meantime, be his help.

Reflection
What is it like being married to you? Are you operating in your role as a helpmate? Are you helping your husband? Or are you hindering him?

Victory Verse
"Your beauty should not come from outward adornment, such as elaborate hairstyles and the wearing of gold jewelry or fine clothes. Rather, it should be that of your inner self, the unfading beauty of a gentle and quiet spirit, which is of great worth in God's sight." 1 peter 3:3-4

Prayer
Father God, in the name of Jesus, help me to understand and truly embrace my role as a suitable helper to my husband. Show me how to be the help he needs. Give me creative and loving ways to encourage and help my husband to inspire him to be all that you created him to be. Amen.

Confession
I am a wife of noble character. My husband's heart safely trusts in me. I am a help to my husband and a blessing in his life. With me by his side, my husband is a mighty man of valor and everything his hands touch is blessed.

Chapter 4

Your Assignment: Pray for Him

"And pray in the Spirit on all occasions with all kinds of prayers and requests. With this in mind, be alert and always keep on praying for all the Lord's people." Ephesians 6:18

Your position as a wife is honorable. God saw that it was not good for man to be alone, and he created woman. You and I are the final touch, the missing link, the icing on the cake, and the blessing to our husbands.

Your husband was not created for you. He was not created to make you happy. Woman was created from man and for man, for companionship, partnership, for support, and help. Your marriage is not about your happiness. In fact, your marriage is not about you.

IT IS YOUR JOB

When you accept a position of employment, you also accept the duties and assignments of the job and the manager for the position you were hired to fill. Your manager or boss is given authority over you. They have authority on purpose. You do not have to like the fact that they have authority over you, but you have to submit to that authority or chance losing your job.

If something does not go right at work, do you get in your feelings? Do you pop off at the mouth to your boss? Do you give your boss a piece of your mind? Do you tell coworkers all of the things you do not like about your boss?

You accepted the wife position. In accepting the position, you also accepted the duties. If your husband asks you to do something, as long as it is not a sin, do it. When your boss asks you to do something, you do not hesitate. Do your best to be as accommodating toward your husband.

This is not about being controlled or told what to do; it is about serving in love. Your husband in essence is your boss, in a respectful manner. He has God-given authority over you. Your husband is your lifetime partner. How can we treat our employers and our boss at work better than we treat our husbands?

You have an assignment as a wife and that needs to be a focal point. Your assignment is not based on whether or not your husband does his part. You are responsible, to God, to do your part no matter what your husband is or is not doing.

I heard an amazing teaching by Minister Chavon Townsel of Men of Acts Ministry. Minister Townsel taught that a wife is to her husband what the Holy Spirit is to the believer. Wow! Did you catch that? You are to your husband what the Holy Spirit is to the believer.

The Holy Spirit serves as a comforter. The Holy Spirit strengthens us. The Holy Spirit intercedes for us. The Holy Spirit is an advocate, a counselor, and an intercessor for us. As wives we are called to help our husbands, serve as comforters to them, strengthen them, counsel them, be their advocate, and intercede for them. How do we accomplish all of this? Prayer.

Your assignment is to pray for your husband. Stop talking about him and stop talking back to him. Start praying for him. There is no way to be successful at marriage or to be successful as a wife without prayer.

The best way to help your husband is to fulfill your assignment to pray for him. You might be the only one praying for him. You are closest to him anyway. You see him regularly. You know things about him that others do not know. You are the perfect candidate to pray for him. It is your job!

THE POWER OF PRAYER

I remember when my prayer partner, Sherry, and I were praying for a breakthrough in my marriage. In my mind, I was plotting to leave my husband. I had one foot in and one foot out. I called Sherry, not to pray for my marriage, but to pray God would help me to leave him. I was tired of arguing and truly felt like we had made a mistake in getting married.

Sherry is seasoned in marriage. She has been married for thirty years, to be exact, so the wisdom she imparted was very real, honest, helpful, and biblical based. During this particular occasion, she told me that she felt God urging us to fast. She told me that God was going to do something big for my marriage, but we absolutely needed to fast.

Sherry and I fasted for 24 hours. My husband was not aware that I was fasting. I could not let him know about my plot to leave him so when he decided that we would attend Saturday prayer at a church we had been visiting, I went along.

The service was being held during the last few hours of the fast.

As the Holy Spirit moved through the prayer service, I noticed my husband becoming emotional. He put his head in hands, and bent over onto his lap, and he wept. I began thanking God silently, trusting He was going to do the big thing my prayer partner prophesied. I was still plotting to leave. I had no idea what the big thing was, but I was desperately believing and trusting God to move.

At the end of prayer, the Pastor opened the floor for questions. My husband hopped to his feet. I thought he had a question to ask. I had my head bowed, my eyes closed, and I was praying. When the Pastor gave my husband the floor to speak, he said, "My wife and I want to join the church." I opened my eyes and lifted my head immediately. My first thought was, "we do?"

I had no idea that he had been contemplating joining the church, but for me this was the big thing my prayer partner had mentioned. This was my breakthrough! I was at the end of my fast and God moved because of the praying and fasted I did with my prayer partner.

Although my husband was a believer, he had not been an active member of a church in over 15 years. This was the first time he joined a church as an adult. We had discussed the idea of joining a church together; however, we both had experienced pain, disappointment, and isolation within the church. So, neither of us had joining a church as our top priority. Although I was caught off guard with my husband's decision for *us* to join the church, when the Pastor motioned for my husband to come to the front of the sanctuary, I grabbed his hand and followed him.

Prayer works. When you directly address God, making reverent petitions and /or showing appreciation and thanks, power is released and activated (or reactivated). When you pray, that is the only time what you share and express is guaranteed to not be repeated or put on blast. You do not have this guarantee when you vent to others about your marriage.

We are in a covenant relationship with our husbands and God. Ecclesiastes 4:12, says a three cord strand is not easily broken. Even if your husband is not doing his part, yet, you do your part. Even if your husband is not praying, you pray. Your connection to God helps hold the marriage together. Your prayers of intercession help make manifest the promises of God in your marriage.

GOD SAID I TALK TOO MUCH

On another occasion, my husband and I attended a church service with my sister, Charmaine, early in our marriage. We did not have a church home of our own at the time. We had been having challenges and because I talked so much my sister was well aware of the challenges within my marriage. Charmaine invited us to the church service because the teaching was about family, dysfunctional family to be exact.

As my husband and I sat next to one another portraying an image of a happy couple, broken, trying to look fixed, the message resonated with me. Forgive me for not remembering and providing the full detail of the message or the scriptures to go along with it. The one thing I recall is being convicted for talking too much.

Right there, in my seat, I felt God telling me I talked too much and I needed to stop. Then, He began showing me that I had talked so much I talked myself out of my own home. Although we sat in the church service together that night, we were not staying under the same roof at the time.

This was during the period where I had painted the ugly picture of my husband to my mother, other family members, and my friends.

I was not operating in my role as a suitable helper and I was not fulfilling my assignment to pray. I was so convicted after the teaching that I had no other choice than to pray and repent. That moment of prayer and repentance sparked the fire that sent me back home and would help turn my marriage around. As I began to pray for my husband, God began to reveal and expose things to me, about me. As things were revealed and I prayed about them I saw the answers to my prayers in different areas.

One area for example pertains to my husband's associations. Remember, in the beginning of my marriage, I wished my husband had made new friends here in California. Well, he started making friends, but not all of them had good intentions. Initially, I fussed and complained about these friends. When my fussing and complaining fell on death ears I began to pray. One by one certain "friends" fell off.

I am not encouraging you to pray away the friends your husband has that you do not like. Some of the friendships we do not like are purposeful in their lives. But if there are any connections that are unhealthy, or only serve as distractions, you and I have every right to tell God about it. No need to fuss or complain to your husband. Go to God and leave it there.

I saw God answer my prayers when I chose to go to Him instead of talking to others. I saw God answer my prayers when I stopped fussing and starting praying. As God showed me that I talked too much, He also showed me the damage I had caused and prompted me to be the one to fix it.

I had to go to my family members and friends and apologize for inviting them into my marriage. I had to ask them to stop speaking negatively about my marriage. I had to pray over and uproot every negative seed I had planted, plus the seeds I allowed others to plant. I had to stop talking and start praying, diligently.

STOP, DROP, AND PRAY

As a wife, you have a mission to pray for your husband. You have been appointed and assigned to talk to God about your husband. Go to God on your husband's behalf. Go to war in the Spirit for your husband. Stand in the gap for him. Now, that is being a suitable helper.

It is difficult to be at odds with someone you are regularly praying for. It is difficult to bad mouth someone you are regularly praying for. It is difficult for someone to continue mistreating you or acting foul when you are regularly praying for them. Stop talking and start praying.

I had never considered myself to be a prayer warrior. I knew the basics about praying and I was confident in my ability to get a prayer through to God. I had prayed for others and had others pray for me, but I had not yet applied what I knew to my marriage.

You may not consider yourself to be a prayer warrior and that is okay. Each of us has different gifts. I encourage you, however to strive to be a praying wife for your husband and marriage. This in turn will bless your family, your finances, and all areas of your life. Learn everything you can about prayer and begin to apply what you learn in your marriage.

For now, I encourage you to begin to look at your husband differently. Feelings aside, make your assignment (and your role) the focus. It is not about the man, your husband; it is about his position as a husband. You chose to marry him and in doing so you chose to accept the role, duty, and assignment of being his wife.

Do not concern yourself with whether or not your husband is, has been, or will do his part. Stop, drop, and pray. Do you know that God has enough power to get your husband to do what He wants Him to do? And if he doesn't do what God wants him to do, God will deal with him. What if it is not about him changing? What if God is waiting on you to change? Stop, drop, and pray.

You are married for purpose, not happiness. If you begin to focus on purpose and not your feelings, you will automatically reap happiness and much more. God wants your husband saved. God wants your husband walking in his purpose. How do I know God wants your husband saved? The Bible says that he wishes that none should perish (2 Peter 3:9).

It is God's will for your husband to be saved and to be walking in his purpose! It is God's will for your husband to take his rightful position as head of his family! It is God's will for your husband to love you as Christ loves the church. It is God's will for your husband to not deal with you harshly, but your husband needs your help. Stop, drop, and PRAY!

Reflection
How often do you pray for your husband? Are your prayers genuinely for his good? Do you talk about your husband more than you pray for him?

Victory Verse
"Therefore, confess your sins to one another and pray for one another, that you may be healed. The prayer of the righteous person has great power as it is working." James 5:16

Prayer
Father God, in the name of Jesus, help me to embrace the assignment to pray for my husband. Show me what to pray for and what to pray about where he is concerned.

Confession
I pray for my husband daily. I am attentive to the Holy Spirit and always know what to pray for concerning my husband. I am confident that God hears my prayers and because I am confident that He hears me, I know that He has answered me.

Chapter 5

Respect: A Mandate

"...and the wife must respect her husband." Ephesians 5:23

  The Bible tells a wife to respect her husband. It does not say he must earn your respect, or he should respect you first. It does not say your husband has to do (fill in the blank) or has to be (fill the blank) before you respect him. In Ephesians 5, it is simple, it is clear, and it is a mandate: "…and the wife must respect her husband."

  Respect means esteem, admire, think highly of, have a high opinion of, hold in high regard, hold in high esteem, look up to, revere, reverence, and honor. We are not called to respect the man or the person, but we are called to respect his role and his position, as husband.

  Have you ever had a boss or a teacher that you did not like? No matter what you thought of that boss or teacher personally, you still respected their position. You do not mouth off at your boss or teacher. You do not stop doing work until they act right. You may even quit the job, or drop the class, if it becomes unbearable, but my point is we tend to treat others better than our husbands. This should not be.

At one point you liked your husband. You made a choice to marry him so he did something right, at some point. Life happens when we get married. Real life. It is very different than dating.

THE STRUGGLE IS REAL

My husband and I had a whirlwind summer romance. We ate out every night, we spent every weekend together, we had fun all of the time, but we also did not live together and my kids were in another state (while I was training for my job). During the dating phase, I did not experience the impact of child support coming out of his check when the light bill was due. We had not slept in the same bed night after night. Our reality was warped so when reality kicked in it was a different ball game.

When you are married you are given an opportunity to see the whole person. You see them at their best. You see them at their absolute worst. You see them on their good days and bad days.

Both of us do not always look good or smell good (I try) after a long day of work or ripping and running. The weave has to be taken out and he has to see you with no makeup. Some days he does not shave or he tries to kiss you and has not brushed his teeth, yet. Bills pile up, kids act out, pets destroy things, and your spouse may even break or destroy things, things that mean a lot to you. Some days you may want to be left alone, completely, but you cannot make him leave.

The point is life gets real once you get married and live together. You will find yourself bothered in some form or fashion by your husband. You will learn things about him that you did not know and you will learn things that you do not like.

Maybe you are a neat person and he is not. Maybe he likes to let the dishes soak and you like to wash them right away. You like the garbage can to be in the backyard, but he wants it in the house. You get cold easily; he likes to sleep with the fan on. All kinds of little things come out or are revealed and you have to find a way to deal with it, accept it, and move forward.

RESPECT IS A CHOICE

In some marriages, wives find themselves losing respect for their husbands based on some of the changes mentioned. They also lose respect due to his action or inaction. Maybe he is not as ambitious as you thought he was. Maybe he is bad with money. Maybe he smokes or drinks, too much, in your opinion. Maybe he curses. Maybe you do not like the music he listens to. Maybe you do not like his friends. Maybe he leaves his socks on the floor in the room or he leaves the toilet seat up habitually. Maybe he cannot seem to keep a job. There are a world of possibilities and maybes. There are many reasons some wives use to justify losing respect for or just not respecting their husbands.

Did you require anything of God before you honored Him? I know that God is God, but did you have requirements of Him before you respected Him? Based on God's position, once you became a believer, you began to follow suit. We respect God because of who He is. We are called to honor (respect) our husbands, because of who they are.

Respect is a choice. Your husband does not have to earn respect for you to give it to him. The Bible tells wives to respect their husbands! Period. You can argue, you can debate, and you can disagree, but the truth of the matter is we are told to respect our husbands.

Stop placing requirements on your husband in order for you to do what God told you to do. There is a divine purpose for the instruction given for wives to honor (respect) their husbands. Do you honor your boss at work? Do you do what your boss asks you to do? If your boss tells you to do something, do you get an attitude? Do you pop off at your boss? Seriously?! If your boss makes a decision that you disagree with, how do you approach them? How can we, as women of God, give more honor to the boss at work than our own husband?

I used to tell my husband my boss did not talk to me the way he did and that is how I could respect my boss more than him. For me, this was a fact, however I am held accountable to do what the Word tells me to do. If I deliberately disobey the Word, especially concerning my marriage, I am out of order. When I am out of order, I am out of position. When I am out of position, my covering is at stake and that leaves room for the enemy.

If your husband does not like something that you do, make an effort to not do it. If your husband asks you to do something, make an effort to do it. If you tell your husband that you will be home by 10 pm, be home by 10 pm, or call if you are running late. We do this for our jobs and sometimes for appointments, why not show the same consideration for our life partner?

Respect is a choice. Be mindful of how you treat your husband. God is always watching. Just like God will deal with your husband for how he treats or mistreats you, God will deal with you for how you treat or mistreat you husband.

Yes, I know he does not seem to always be mindful of how he treats you. Yes, I understand he may talk to you crazy and disrespect you. We are not talking about him, we are talking about you. I am attempting to help you get in alignment so that God can move and you can experience a fulfilling marriage.

YOUR CONDUCT AND BEHAVIOR

Your conduct represents your husband. Your conduct represents God. What you do, where you go, what you say, how you dress, what you post on social media, who you follow on social media, your overall presentation represents your husband and God. How are you representing?

As women of faith, we should seek to please God and our husbands with our behavior. This is a part of respecting and honoring our husbands. If you are snappy and rude towards your husband in the grocery store, is that a display of love and respect? If you are all up in another man's face blushing and laughing at work, is that a display of love and respect towards your husband? If you are drooling over photos shared on social media of a half dressed man, is that a display of love and respect towards your husband?

The Bible says to avoid the very appearance of evil (1 Thessalonians 5:22). We have to be alert and aware of our conduct and presentation in the presence of our husbands. We have to be alert and aware of our conduct and presentation when our husbands are not present.

When you spend money on something that your husband is unaware of, are you respecting him? When those boxes from Amazon come in and we unpack them, hide or put away the contents, and get rid of the box so he will not know, is that respect? Do not get me wrong, some husbands are okay with things like this. You have to know what your husband is not okay with and do your best to work with that.

The Bible tells us to submit to our husbands as unto the Lord. If God tells you to stop spending so much, are you going to listen? If your husband tells you to stop spending so much, are you going to listen? Submit to your husband, as you would to God. It is not always easy and I get that. The ultimate goal is to be pleasing to God and to obey His word.

SOCIAL MEDIA

I am a member of several groups for married women on Facebook. The groups were generally created with a purpose to provide support and encouragement to wives. A couple of the groups uphold their integrity and truly exist for their intended purpose. However, I have noticed a trend in a few of these groups: Wives talk way too much!

Some of the wives share things about their husbands that blow my mind. I have read about husbands cheating, their performance in the bedroom, their hygiene habits, and more. There are wives involved in extramarital affairs, they have children who may not belong to their husband, and they share these things on social media, with strangers.

I completely understand feeling the need to vent. I have been there. I completely understand wanting to get things off of your chest. I have done that. It is absolutely disrespectful, however when we expose our husbands, especially before strangers.

It is one thing to generalize what is shared or posted in these groups. It is another ball game when a hurting or angry wife puts her husband on blast. When this happens, seeds are being planted. These strange women, who call one another "sister" all day long, are sometimes adding fertilizer to the seeds planted.

I have literally witnessed a post from one group being screenshot and posted into another group. Now, even more women know that the husband is cheating or having performance issues in the bedroom. I often wonder if any of these posts ever get back to the husbands. Imagine if they did?! Ouch.

Respect is a choice, ladies. The Bible advises us to seek Godly counsel (Proverbs 24:6). Some of us are so caught up in trends and the ways of the world that we are entangling ourselves and our marriages in mess.

For example, by the time the wife resolved her issues with her husband; other wives are still commenting and sharing her post. There are people still stirring up what we may have put to rest. Do you understand what I mean?

Listen, some of these social media groups are great. Sometimes we need support beyond our immediate circle or family. I get it. I was there. We must, however, learn to have boundaries that help to guard and protect our marriages.

It is disrespectful to your husband for you to put his business in the streets and all over social media. It is wrong and out of order to confide in potentially thousands of people you do not know about something your husband has a right to know. YOU TALK TOO MUCH!!! Stop, drop, and PRAY! Take your concerns, frustrations, issues, and questions to God!

If we spent as much time praying as we do reading about other people's business and sharing our own, the state of marriages would improve. For those of us who do not participate in this behavior, yet we see it daily, help the other wives. Encourage them with the Word, feed them scriptures, and advise them to stop making their business public.

We have to help one another, the right way. We have to support and encourage one another with the Truth, not our opinions. We have to show respect to God and our husbands with our conduct, on and offline. Respect is a choice!

INSUBORDINATION

My family is blended. I entered my marriage with two sons; my husband entered our marriage with a daughter. I am very protective of my sons. I went through an ugly divorce in the past and it really damaged my oldest son who is now 20 years old. Naturally, I am a shield over my youngest son, who is 10 years old.

My bonus daughter was only two years old when my husband and I were married. In my opinion, my husband did not have enough parenting experience to tell my son what to do. Early in our marriage, we bumped heads about this. Anytime he told my son to do anything, I had something to say or I would undermine his authority as a parent. Was this a display of love and respect towards my husband? Absolutely not.

God is not the author of confusion and He honors order. You are mandated to respect your husband, right where he is. He may be broken. He may be blind. He may be ill-equipped. He may be out of order. He may have no direction. You chose to marry him! Buck against the system that God has put into place, if you want to, but you will continue to block blessings that are assigned to your marriage.

Honor your husband! Think highly of your husband! He may not be all that you expected and he may fall short, often. I am sure if we ask him he would agree that you are not all that he expected and you fall short, too. Isn't it great that we serve such an awesome God that even when we fall short He still loves us?

Love your husband, ladies. Encourage him. Respect him. Honor him. Help him. Pray for him. Be his peace. Do not be the wife who kills her husband from the inside out. Be the wife who is in tune with her man and builds him up because she is connected to and led by God.

Do not interrupt him when he is talking. Do not try to over talk him. Do not cross your arms and get tight-jaw when he is speaking to you. Do not roll your eyes. Do not undermine his authority. Do not mumble under your breath while he is talking. Would you do any of this to your boss or manager at work?

Your husband is not your child. You may think that he acts like one from time to time, but that is not your business. Your business is to help him, pray for him, and respect him. Respect him like you would any other adult. Look him in the eye when he is talking or when you are talking to him. Do not be rude. Listen to him. Seek to understand him. Do everything you can to respect your husband, not because he deserves it, but because God has mandated you to.

MEN GET TIRED, TOO

Ladies, I know that sometimes marriage takes a lot of work. Sometimes it seems as if all of the work is on us. Sometimes we want our husbands to take the lead, take the initiative, apologize first, take some of the weight off of our shoulders, etc. Sometimes we get tired. Well, men get tired, too.

I am not dismissing your tired or my own. God sees what you do. God will honor your effort and obedience. Just trust Him.

Men often deal with things we are not aware of or know little about. Your husband may be upset, moody, or irritable and he is unkind towards you. There are many times when he is unkind towards you over something you have nothing to do with. His mood, his unkindness, his attitude may have nothing to do with you at all, yet you fall on the receiving end because you are the closest one to him.

The more you pray and work on you the more the Holy Spirit will guide you and show you when to speak, how to speak, and what to say. God will reveal things to you to help you understand or to simply have you to pray. Men often deal with things that we do not understand as women. If your man works outside of the home, he carries the weight of that daily. He may deal with traffic, coworkers, stress, racism, the pressure to provide, live up to a standard, and more. He may be facing or dealing with feelings of inadequacy, low self-esteem, fear, insecurity, etc. These questions were presented in Chapter 2, but I will ask again. Are you a safe place for your husband to come to? Can his heart safely trust in and confide in you?

Some of our husbands are not where we are spiritually. Some of them do not go to church. Some of them do not pray. Some of them disagree with paying tithes or taking communion. Some of them do not believe at all or anymore. Whatever it is about your husband, your job is to pray. Respect where he is on his journey and remember you did not start off where you are.

Everyone has coping mechanisms or ways in which we deal with things. Some of us have developed the habit of complaining or venting to help us cope. Some of us have habits that began as coping mechanisms, like eating sweets, biting your nails, exercising, binging on television, walking, and so on. Just like we have developed ways to cope, our husbands have as well.

Before judging or criticizing your husband for the way he copes, seek to understand him. If he has habits that you disagree with, he knows by now that you do not like it. Do not bring it up to him anymore. Go to God and trust God to turn things around in His time. Sometimes the habits are simply coping behaviors that your husband learned well before you were in his life. The more pressure we put on them about these things the easier it is for them to continue doing them.

Lack of respect will push your husband to activate his coping mechanism.

Habits die hard. They die, eventually, but it takes work and it takes time. Do not fuss at your husband about his habits. Do not fuss at your husband about anything. Fussing does not lead to accomplishment or change. Respect where he is and pray for him.

Men get tired of being strong. Men get tired of the pressure. Men get tired of our mouths. Men get tired, just like we do.

The responsibility of being a husband is huge. Think about that for a moment. Your husband has authority over you and is accountable for you. If you have children, he is also responsible and accountable for them. I know you do a lot, too. I know you carry things that become heavy. I know it is hard to bite your tongue when he is being rude or disrespectful. Do not worry about that. Show your husband God is alive and real inside of you by how you treat and respond to him.

God has expectations of your husband. He has a tall order to fill. Your husband is mandated to love you, as Christ loves the church. That is a lot of love! Your husband having headship is a huge responsibility but know that he is accountable to God.

DRAW HIM CLOSER

Men are drawn to people who respect them. Their primary need is respect. We must lace our words with love and kindness for them to receive what we have to say when it is time to say something. We must model behavior consistent with the Word of God in front of our husbands. We must step out of the way, stay in our lane, do our part, and give our husbands room to do theirs.

Our role as a wife is powerful. We were created with great influence. Just remember the story of the Garden of

Eden. Eve had influence on Adam. Her influence was so strong that she led her husband to sin with her. Our influence can steer our men in the right direction or the wrong one. We can make or break someone with our mouths and sometimes with the way we look at them. Will you use your power and influence to build up your man or tear him down? Will you be his peace or the constant nagging drip of an old leaking pipe?

Draw your husband closer to you by respecting him. Do not be the foolish woman who tears her house down with her own hands. Do not be the one to slice and dice your man with your mouth. He may be jobless, right now. You may make more money than he does, right now. He may have habits you disagree with and addictions that you hate. You married him and you are mandated to respect him.

You are going to have to pray. You are going to have to fast. You are going to have to stand and having done all, keep standing on the Word of God.

What did you think was meant by 'suitable helper?' Did you think you were just created to help decorate the house, look pretty, put together a tasty meal, and be a trophy on his arm? That is not help! Help involves work and the greatest work you can do is spiritual.

Your husband may be in a good place spiritually or he may have no sense of spirituality about him. It is not your job to change him or to convince him to change, especially with your mouth. It is not your job to judge him or to condemn him, either. Remember, your job is to help him, pray for him, and respect him.

Reflection
Do you believe God knows what He is doing in your marriage? Do you trust God enough to do what He says? Are you respecting your husband as the Bible advises?

Victory Verse
"Be devoted to one another in love. Honor one another above yourselves." Romans 12:10

Prayer
Father God, in the name of Jesus, forgive me for being disrespectful to my husband. You have placed my husband in authority over me on purpose. I trust you to lead me through my husband and I trust you to lead my husband, regardless of where he is in his walk with you. Amen.

Confession
I respect my husband. I show proper respect to him when we are together and when we are apart. My conduct and behavior is pleasing to God and because of my obedience I am blessed.

Chapter 6

Sex & Intimacy

"The wife does not have authority over her own body but yields it to her husband. In the same way, the husband does not have authority over his own body but yields it to his wife." 1 Corinthians 7:4

Your body is not your own, anymore. After marriage, the Bible says that the two shall become one (Mark 10:8). As a wife, you no longer have control over your body. This is a tough subject for me because I am a survivor of sexual abuse. I was a molested as a young girl, by friends of the family, while spending the night away from home. As a preteen, I was sexually assaulted and as teenager I was sexually assaulted, again. As an adult, sexual abuse plagued my life, once more.

LET'S TALK ABOUT SEX…OR NOT

Sex to me never equated love. Even when love was present in a relationship, if sex was present, it was detached from love altogether. As a result of sexual abuse, I found myself fornicating as a teenager. I gave myself to those I was in relationships with as a way of avoiding them ever having to take it from me. I was not promiscuous, in my mind; I simply took the initiative to give the men in my life what I thought they wanted. If I gave it away, no one could take it away, and I was in control, right?

Imagine having this mind set and then going into my marriage. When my husband and I got married I did not know that my sexual abuse history was still a problem for me. I thought I had healed and I thought none of that would affect my relationships any longer.

My husband likes to talk about sex. Talking about sex with him was uncomfortable, for me. He would ask questions that I did not want to answer and he could not understand why. The more questions he asked, the more disconnected I became emotionally. The problem is women generally have to be connected emotionally to physically enjoy sex.

In the beginning, my sex life with my husband was great. Yet, his questions continued, therefore I continued to disconnect. As a result of disconnecting, I did not enjoy sex with my husband after a while.

Sex was a chore for me. It was a part of what I knew I was supposed to do as a wife, but not something I really wanted to do. This was during a time when we were not getting along well. I would pray before, during, and after sex. Before sex, I was praying my husband did not want it. During sex, I was praying he would hurry up. After sex, I was praising God that it was over.

A few months into my marriage sex started to hurt. The first few times I thought it was just me, but there were occasions where I was brought to tears because I was in a lot of pain. Initially, it seemed like my husband did not understand me or what I was going through. I did not understand me or what I was going through, but as I began to pray (yes, it is okay to pray about sex with your husband), things began to change.

My husband would approach me for sex. You know, they have their own way of asking or hinting at wanting to go there. Most of the time, I had a long explanation about why I did not want to do it. I would use my gift of talking to explain my way out of it. I would go into detail about my body hurting or being physically tired.

Yes, my body did hurt 99% of the time when I said it did. Deep within, however, I was also disconnected emotionally and just did not want to be intimate. Mind you, this was during the period that my husband and I were arguing about almost everything. My response and my talking during those moments of him approaching me often shut him down and turned him away.

There were times when I was upset with my husband and did not want him to touch me. It was bad enough sex seemed like a chore to me and has never equated to love. But when he upset me or did something or said something that I did not like, this only pushed me away further. I would roll over and away from him. Every time he touched me I pulled away or popped his hand. Imagine how many frustrating nights this caused both of us, especially him.

If you withhold sex from your husband as a form of punishment, you are out of order. The Bible says, that we no longer have authority over our bodies and we are to only withhold sex if both husband and wife agree and for the purpose of fasting. Sex was not intended to be used to manipulate or to control our husbands.

When you take something and misuse it for the wrong purpose, you distort it. Distortion, in this case, can open the door to pornography and infidelity. No, I am not saying if a husband cheats under these circumstances that it is your fault.

At the same time, there is a reason the Bible tells us not to withhold sex from one another. That reason is temptation. When you open a door for the enemy, he will come racing in and do whatever he can to destroy your marriage. Do not give the enemy any room!

DIAGNOSED AND SUBMITTED

After a few months of experiencing painful intercourse, I made an appointment to see my Doctor. My Doctor was unable to detect anything by visual and basic physical examination so she sent me to a specialist. Prior to going to the specialist, I had Googled my symptoms. I had self-diagnosed myself and shared the information with my husband.

Low and behold, the specialist diagnosed me with a condition that was in fact causing painful intercourse. The condition was classified as an autoimmune disorder. It is uncommon and the cause is unknown. It is suggested that an overactive immune system or a hormonal imbalance may be the cause or play a role. It is not contagious and cannot be spread through sexual intercourse. The main side effect is painful sex.

In Genesis 1:28, God told Adam and Eve to be fruitful and multiply. Sex between husband and wife is a tool to reproduce. The act of reproduction was also intended to be pleasurable. There are sensors in our body that cause us to feel pleasure and these sensors are within and around our reproductive organs, so the two go together. We are supposed to have sex with our husbands and we should enjoy it. I was not enjoying it, however.

I had no idea what was wrong with me or how to fix it until I prayed. I could not understand why this rare condition was a part of my life. In my heart, I wanted to enjoy sex with my husband, again. I wanted to be pleasing and enjoy the overall experience, but I did not know how to talk to him about it.

Many nights I had a headache. It was not an excuse, I literally had a headache. Instead of telling my husband I had a headache, I would pray and submit. Believe it or not my headache would go away, after the encounter. In those moments where my body hurt or I did not feel like having sex, after it was all said and done I would feel better and so would he.

I had to go to God. I had to face my stuff and then invite the Holy Spirit into the bedroom. Yes, I said invite the Holy Spirit into the bedroom. For me, inviting the Holy Spirit created an atmosphere we needed in our bedroom. Instead of discomfort and tension, there was now comfort and peace. With the presence of comfort and peace, I was able to give myself to my husband without reservation and without physical pain.

JUST DO IT

A sister-wife of mine, Tenisha, shared a confession of faith about sex with me. The first time I read the confession of faith, I felt charged and motivated. I was excited and eager to see the changes in my life. I purposed in my heart and mind to read the confession in hopes that it would help my sex life within my marriage.

As I began to read the confession, it changed my thinking and my heart. As a result, the sexual encounters between my husband and I changed, as well. There were times when I felt prompted to go home and have sex with my husband or to join him in the shower and I followed suit. These promptings and my obedience helped changed the tone of sex within our marriage.

Just like other areas within my marriage I had to learn to take the topic of sex to God. Eventually, I got to a place where instead of responding to my husband, I would pray. I would then submit myself to him and have sex at times when I did not want to.

Sex is a connector. It brings two people closer together, emotionally, mentally, spiritually, and physically. Sex is the language of love, within marriage. Your husband needs sex from you, just as much as he needs your respect, prayers, and help.

The fact that your husband desires you is huge. There are some marriages where the husband no longer desires his wife, for whatever reason. If that is your situation, I have included the confession of faith on sex that changed my life, for you, towards the back of this book (the confession has been altered from its original state). If there are any issues of complications currently plaguing your sex life within your marriage this confession will help you. I started reading the confession daily and within the first week, our sexual encounters were fire, if you know what I mean.

Sex with our husbands should be enjoyable and fun even. In that moment, two are becoming one, literally. Hormones and chemicals in the body are activated and released that help bring you and your husband closer together. There is a connection or supposed to be, on all levels. Like with every other area within our marriage, we have to pray and trust God about sex.

Your situation may not be as extreme as mine. In addition, to sexual abuse I had health issues that were causing sex to be painful. After the specialist diagnosed me, I knew what to pray about and what to pray against. I used natural remedies to help soothe my discomfort and I claimed my healing, by faith. I confessed my healing and it has been months since I have experienced pain during sex.

Why am I sharing all of this? A change in our bodies as women is a real thing. Men go through changes as well, but I think women go through more. We cannot allow the changes that occur in our bodies to impact our marriage in a negative manner. We serve a mighty God. We serve a God who is still in the business of healing.

I do not believe that it is God's will that a husband and wife should not be able to have enjoyable sex. Although my husband and I experienced the not enjoyable part, I am thankful I was able to pray through it and eventually out of it. As women, as our body changes, we have to pray for God to help us communicate with our husbands.

Men do not understand what it is like to be our kind of tired. They do not understand what it is like to be on your cycle, about to start it, or coming off of it, and just not wanting to be bothered. It is generally hormonal; however they do not understand that we sometimes need time for the hormones to balance.

What am I saying to you? Sex is as important to our husbands as respect is. They need respect (they need help) and they need sex. Once again, when we accepted the role of wife we accepted everything that came with it. Having sex with your husband is a part of being married.

OBEDIENCE AND HEALING

If this is a difficult or challenging area for you, like it was for me, watch what you say. This is definitely not a topic we should be running to our girlfriends or social media about. When you pray however, God may lead you or connect you with someone who can help you. It was God who connected me to Tenisha and without giving her details she shared the confession of faith on sex and it was life changing for me.

I am sharing my personal experience, with the agreement and approval of my husband, to help someone else. What helped me during this challenging period was focusing on the fact that my body is not my own and being right before God. In my doing this, God began to show my husband that

I was not making excuses or simply pushing him away. There was something physical going on and it had to be dealt with. I believe that my obedience is what cleared the path for my healing to manifest and my husband's ability to understand.

What does this have to do with talking too much? I tried to explain things to my husband about my body that he was not getting. Even after the specialist told him and shared the diagnosis with him, it just did not register completely. Also, my husband did not understand my history of sexual abuse. In an effort to understand he would ask questions but I took offense to his questions and eventually did not want to discuss the topic with him anymore.

This can be a sensitive and challenging topic for some. As with other areas within or marriage we have to consult God. I could not make my husband understand how I felt, but God could. When my husband wanted sex and I did not, because I prayed and submitted, I believe God supernaturally prevented the pain from affecting me. My continued obedience and diligent prayers resulted in my healing.

I am not telling any wife to lie down and be a sex slave to your husband. What I am encouraging you to do is to pray. Sex was intended to be pleasurable for both husband and wife. Sex was intended to be common and regular between husband and wife. We should enjoy sex with our husbands. We should desire plenty of sex with our husbands. If this is missing, something is going on and it needs to be addressed.

Reflection

Is there something in your past that impacts your sexual relationship with your husband? Does your health affect your desire to have sex? Do you withhold sex from your husband as a form of punishment or control?

Prayer

Father God, in the name of Jesus, forgive me for withholding sex from my husband for any reason. Your Word says that my body is no longer my own, just as my husband's body is no longer his. Renew the sexual intimacy and experience between my husband and I. Give us a burning, unquenchable desire for one another. Amen

Confession

I love my husband. I desire my husband and my husband desires me. My bosom satisfies my husband all of the days of his life His heart is turned towards me and my heart is turned towards him.

Chapter 7

Be Intentional

"But I tell you that everyone will have to give account on the Day of Judgment for every empty word spoken."
Matthew 12:36

Most of us did not count up the cost when we said "for better or worse." We did not consider all that could be included with "worse." You and I took a vow. We looked our husbands in the eye, in the presence of a witness or witnesses and made an oath, a pledge, a promise, a commitment, a covenant, a guarantee. You did not write your vow, or maybe you did, but we all spoke our vow.

On that beautiful day of love, we were not concerned with the meaning of "better or worse." We were not concerned with anything other than getting married. Ladies, we vowed to our husbands in the presence of God. Ponder that for a moment. Think back on your wedding vows and what you actually committed to in the presence of God. These words may be exact or similar to your vow:

"I _____, take thee, _____, to be my wedded husband, to have and to hold, from this day forward, for better, for worse, for richer, for poorer, in sickness and in health, to love and to cherish, till death do us part."

You are accountable for every word you speak. Words have creative power. We shape our world with our words. The Bibles says that life and death are in the power of the tongue! If you knew how powerful your words are you would never speak a thoughtless word again! In fact, I challenge you to begin to seriously think before you speak. Pause before your respond. Pause before you begin to talk, about anything.

YOUR POWER OF INFLUENCE

Women are natural influencers. We have the power to build up or tear down with our mouths, our words. Have you ever given someone a good cursing out? I mean the kind of cursing that makes them shut up because you hit a nerve and told the truth, in a strong, powerful, yet degrading manner? Yes, degrading. When we curse someone out, we demote with our words. We decapitate with our words. We make others feel very small or invisible with our words.

How many times have we snapped at our husbands? How many times have we spoken hurtful words to them? How many times have we spoken ill of them to others? We have degraded our husbands. We have attempted to demote them. We cut them on the inside. We planted negative seeds into their lives and our own.

Do you not know that every negative word (seed) you plant in your husband's life is going to pour over into your life as well? Last time I checked, the Bible says that the two shall become one. If we are one in the eyes of God and we curse our husbands, we are cursing ourselves, too.

I was on the verge of giving up on my marriage. I was not praying regularly or with authority. I was not reading the Word. My Bible was literally dusty from sitting on the shelf closed. I was not confessing anything other than negativity, doubt, and my every frustration.

I was not new to Christian faith when I married my husband. We are both believers and we were believers when we met. We were both saved, sanctified, and filled with the Holy Spirit, when we met. We fasted before we decided to get married. We prayed on our first date, remember? We prayed just about every day after the first date until I left Florida to return to California. During our Skype and Facebook Messenger video calls, we would pray. Up and until my husband relocated to California we tried to live right.

Here we were, two believers, with authority, yet denying the power. I thought I had married the wrong man. He thought he had married the wrong woman. I spoke against my marriage and my husband. He spoke against me and our marriage, also.

The negativity I spoke and sowed caused a lot of damage within my family. It also soured the view of my husband to my family and friends. I had prayed for them to like whomever I married, yet I caused them to dislike him with my mouth and my words. My influence was powerful!

I had to apologize to my husband. I had to intentionally ask my husband for forgiveness. Not by text or over the telephone. Not by a letter. I had to look him eye to eye and apologize. I apologized for not truly knowing or understanding my role. I apologized for disrespecting him and talking about him.

Ladies, apologize to your husband and ask him for forgiveness. You may think that he owes you an apology. He probably does, but I encourage you to go first. Be intentional. Position yourself to be in right standing with God. Forgive your husband if you need to and certainly apologize. Even if you do not feel like you have done anything wrong, humble yourself and apologize just to make sure you have a clean slate with your husband.

You may have hurt him or disrespected him, unknowingly. Check in with him. Apologize to clear the air and ask him if he will forgive you (especially if you have specific things that you are apologizing for). Remember, this is not your boyfriend or some random guy. This is your lifetime partner. You made a vow to this man. Is he not worth you humbling yourself and apologizing?

It does not matter what he has done. This is about you making things right and positioning yourself to be in right standing with God. This is about you and the power of influence that you have on your husband.

Your husband may owe you several apologies. Let God deal with that. Believe me when I tell you that an apology is so much sweeter when God prompts it. Allow God to prompt your husband to apologize to you. If you never receive an apology, do not hold it against your husband or God. Let it go.

SET YOUR INTENTIONS

We have to make up in our minds to be intentional, especially with our words. Have you ever been told if you do not have anything good to say, then do not say anything? Stop biting back. Stop clapping back. Stop popping off when it comes to your husband.

Shut up and pray! Right there in the midst of whatever is going on, pause and pray. God can hear you, even while your husband is talking.

I am not saying to ignore your husband. That is disrespectful. I am saying when he comes at you and you know the angle he is coming from is not love and peace, right then and there pray. It can be as simple as "God help" or "Holy Spirit intervene." When you do open your mouth to speak, use the power of influence that God has given you. Speak with authority in Christ. Speak with confidence. Speak life. Speak intently.

Choose what you are creating. Create peace. Create love. Create connection. The Bible says, that a soft answer turns away wrath (Proverbs 15:1). Your response can kill an argument! Be soft. Be gentle. Be kind intentionally. Be your husband's help when he may have stepped out of the spirit and into the flesh. Be the wise woman who builds her house.

If your husband is lacking, falling short, or if there is anything that you think is missing in him, create it. Yes, CRE-ATE it! Call those things that are not, as though they were (Romans 4:17)! Not only do you have a gift of influence but you have a gift of creativity! You can create with your mouth.

Remember, in the beginning, in Genesis 1:3, when God was creating the earth, He spoke. God said, "Let there be light," and what happened? There was light! God has given us the power to speak and to see what we speak manifest, as long as it is in line with His will.

CHANGE BEGINS WITH YOU

Sometimes we are waiting on God to change our husbands when God is waiting on us to change. I had a hard time with this. I am a strong willed and strong minded woman. I was a single mother for over 17 years. I was raised in a single parent home. My family was primarily matriarchal. As long as I can remember it was me, my mother, my granny, and my auntie. My granny got married and so did my auntie, but I drew my strength from the women long before the men came on the scene.

I learned how to become a runner. When I did not like something in a relationship I would end it. I would leave. I would run. When I did not like something at a job, I would end it. I would leave. I would run.

In my first marriage when things became too much I ended it, I left, I ran. In my current marriage, I tried to repeat the same behavior, but not intentionally. Then, it seemed like God was not allowing me to run anymore. So I started fighting.

When the heat turned up, I turned up, too. I started fighting in the flesh. My husband struggled with anger (did I mention he is a US Marine Veteran?) and I could have had victory over that spirit of anger right away had I fought God's way.

The Bible says that a soft answer turns away wrath, right? Oh but when my husband got angry, I became angrier. If he got loud, I became louder. Our home became a battlefield instead of a place of refuge and peace.

To make matters worse the spirit of anger that he struggled with, attacked me, in a different way. I became violent, aggressive, mean, and evil. I started breaking things, throwing things, and swinging at my husband.

It went from feeling very unnatural to feeling good. I scared myself after I busted a window with my right fist and enjoyed the feeling. I knew then that things were completely out of control and I needed to remove myself from the situation.

My husband played a part, too, but I am talking about me so that I can help you. I had to reflect inward and take a good look at myself. I had to look at what I was doing and not doing. I had to humble myself before God and work on myself.

This time, I left my home and was away for almost three weeks. I had left before, but never stayed away for longer than two or three days. This time was not patty cake. Things were out of control and only God could fix it.

Toward the end of my time away from my home, I stopped by the house to get one of my business suits because I had a job interview. Yes, honey, I was about to get a job and get a new place and move on with my life (two snaps and a circle).

Adultery had not infiltrated our marriage. According to my husband, I had no Biblical right to leave or to divorce him. But I was tired. I was tired of arguing, fussing, going to bed mad, etc. So I left.

The day I stopped by my house to get one of my business suits that I had left behind, my husband asked if we could talk. I told him we could pray.

In that moment, we got down on our knees, together, in front of the couch and prayed. We cried out to God asking for forgiveness and asking Him to help us with our marriage. We had hurt one another with our words and with some actions. We had sown negative seeds into the soil of our own marriage. We had invited other people to sow negative seeds into the soil of our marriage.

That moment of prayer was life changing for my husband and me. It did not fix any problems and it did not stop any disagreements. That moment of prayer, however invited God back into His creation, His design, our marriage.

We intentionally went to God before we were married. We unintentionally left God out during the rough patches. We had to intentionally invite God back into our marriage and trust Him to lead the way.

BE THE BIGGEST FAN OF YOUR MARRIAGE

There are enough people hoping your marriage does not work, the last thing you need is to join them. You have to be your biggest advocate in your marriage. You have to decide that divorce is not an option and will not be used as a threat or an escape.

You have to become intentional about what you speak and when you can help it what others speak. Your marriage is precious. Protect it. Stop gossiping about your marriage. Stop talking about your husband to others. In the end, you look like the fool anyway because you are talking about this man and telling someone his shortcomings and faults, yet you are the one married to him. So just stop.

Your husband is not your enemy. You and your husband are on the same team. I do not care how it looks or how it seems. As long as you are married, you are on the same team. Whether or not your husband is walking in his rightful position as head of the house and doing what he is supposed to do or not, you still have a role, a duty and an assignment you are responsible for.

Invite (or re-invite) God into your marriage. He created marriage and He should be a part of it. Cast your cares on God. Take your concerns, issues, frustration, etc. to God. Be intentional about what you speak. Be intentional about what you do. Be intentional about your marriage.

Reflection
Is there something that you need to ask your husband forgiveness for? Are you willing to go first, and make an effort to make amends with your husband? Are you ready to be intentional within your marriage?

Victory Verse
"Even as I try to please everyone in every way. For I am not seeking my own good but the good of many, so that they may be saved." 1 Corinthians 10:33

Prayer
Father God, in the name of Jesus, think into my thoughts and speak through my words. Help me to think before I speak and to speak only words that encourage and edify. Amen.

Confession
I am intentional with my mouth and my words. I bless others when I speak. I encourage others when I speak. I give hope when I speak. I speak in love.

Chapter 8

Silent Warrior

"For the weapons of our warfare are not carnal, but mighty through God to the pulling down of strongholds." 2 Corinthians 10:4

I met my mother-in-law a week after I met my husband. We spoke over the telephone the day before we met in person. There was an instant connection between us and our relationship has been a blessing.

My husband, who was just a guy I had met at the time, handed me his cellphone. The first thing my mother-in-law said to me was, "I have been praying for God to send my son his wife." She knew before meeting me face to face and before him and I knew that God had ordained our meeting.

JUST PRAY

My relationship with my mother-in-law is amazing and has been from the beginning. We would spend hours on the telephone talking about faith and sharing stories. I went to visit her without my husband and often call her on my own. She really took the time to get to know me and make sure I had the chance to get to know her.

As challenges developed in my marriage, I shared them with my mother-in-law. I sometimes told her more than I told my mother or my girlfriends. I figured she was a safe place for me to vent my frustrations about my husband because she was not going to go tell anyone else what I told her. She was also not going to harbor any ill will toward her son.

No matter what I shared with my mother-in-law, she always encouraged me to pray and fed me scriptures. I am sure some of the things I shared with her were disturbing and hard to digest, but she listened to me. She was never judgmental. She did not take sides and if I was wrong in the matter, she would gently correct me with the Word of God.

There were times when I would text her a mini book, airing my frustration. Her only response would be, "Pray." Conversation after conversation, my mother-in-law encouraged me to silently pray. She used the term "silent warrior" as she would describe what I needed to do as a wife.

Again and again she would advise me to become silent and to pray. She encouraged me to not argue with my husband and to allow God to fight the battle. Be silent and pray.

There were times when I thought she had to have some advice for me, woman to woman, or mother to mother, or mother to daughter. I was convinced that prayer could not be the all in all. But her answer to everything remained the same - pray.

I even went to my father-in-law for advice. Someone had to see what I saw and agree with me. I told my father-in-law some of my frustrations and would text him when his son, my husband, was not acting right. I figured if he will not listen to me or his mother, I know he was going to listen to his dad.

Well, my father-in-law was disappointed and displeased with what I told him. He was not happy about any of it. Yet, he also advised me to pray.

He instructed me to pray with my husband before he went to work each morning. He advised me to make sure we never went to bed upset or with our backs turned to one another. He emphasized that prayer was my best bet.

THE BIRTH OF A SILENT WARRIOR

Frustrated and at my wits end, I began to apply what I had been advised. I slowly started seeing changes and that inspired me to continue being silent and to continue praying. My mother-in-law reminded me that I am a prayer warrior and in this season I needed to be a silent warrior.

Remember, I shared that I thought I had to pray out loud to be effective. I never considered myself to be a prayer warrior. I liked to talk, so hearing myself pray gave me strength and fired me up. However, becoming a prayer warrior was not my goal.

My mother-in-law was gently guiding me to a deeper level of prayer. This was a personal, heartfelt, focused, faith-filled prayer. This was the prayer of a silent warrior.

A warrior is a fighter. A warrior is someone who shows or has courage. A silent warrior is one who fights in the spirit. It is one who knows the power of their words and knows when to speak and when to be quiet. This does not mean you never speak up or that you lose your voice. It simply means that you apply wisdom and seek to remain in tune with the Holy Spirit.

In my secret place, when I was alone, I began to pray. I began to pray like I had never prayed before. I prayed over my home, while my husband and son were not home. I prayed over their clothes and personal items. I prayed inside of my husband's car. I anointed his shoes with oil. I anointed his pillow with oil. I prayed daily and throughout the day.

As a silent warrior no one had to know I was praying. As a silent warrior no one had to know I was fighting, in the spirit. As a silent warrior, my mother, my friends, and even my in-laws did not have to know I was fighting, silently. This was a private journey.

During this period, my spiritual sense was heightened. God would allow me to see and know things I could only know by the Holy Spirit. There were times when I would become emotional while praying until I heard God say, "Get your heart out of it and focus on the assignment." In other words, God was telling me to get out of my feelings and focus on my role, my assignment, and my purpose in my husband's life. Then, God told me to pray diligently for my husband's soul for 30 days straight. My husband was already a believer, but I listened and began the 30 days of life changing prayer for my husband.

THE CHALLENGE

This is your call to become a silent warrior. I challenge you to commit to 30 days of prayer for your husband. Pray for his salvation, his soul, his heart, his mind, his healing, his deliverance, his career, his role as a husband, his role as a father (if applicable), his purpose, and anything else God puts on your heart.

I challenge you already knowing the benefits of doing this challenge. You will have developed a routine of spending time with God, in prayer. You will hear clearer from God. Angels will be dispatched on your behalf to rearrange things and help usher promises, answers, and manifestations. God will work on your husband's heart as you pray.

There is absolutely no harm in taking 30 days to commit to prayer with the focus being your husband. He has authority over you. Praying for him is the best thing you can do for him.

As a believer, you have authority. God is greater in you than anything or anyone in this world. You have direct access to God because of and through Jesus. Take up your cross. Put on the whole armor of God so that you can fight off the fiery arrows aimed at you from the enemy.

Things may be going good for you right now and your marriage may be intact. Your husband may be on track. But do not think the enemy will sit around and just allow that. He is devising a plan against you as you read this book. He is waiting for an opportunity to stir up some mess. If you do not need to take the challenge for your own husband or marriage at this time, that is great. Take the challenge anyway and pray for someone else's marriage for 30 days straight.

I DECLARE WAR

Wives, you have one of the most powerful weapons to use to fight for your marriage – the Bible. The Bible is known as the sword of the spirit. A sword symbolizes power, protection, authority, strength and courage. If our warfare is not against flesh and blood, then it is spiritual. If our fight is spiritual, then we have to fight using spiritual tools.

I declare WAR!

I summons the Godly warrior inside of you and I encourage you to align yourself up with the Word. Start today to walk in your role and to fulfill your assignment. Position yourself to receive all that God has in store for you and your marriage. Honor your husband's role and operate in a meek and quiet spirit, which is pleasing to God.

To the wives who are strong in faith right now, to the wives who fully understand their spiritual right and authority, to the wives who are filled with the Holy Spirit with the evidence of speaking in tongues, to the wives who are intercessors and prayer warriors....

We are under attack! Our sisters are under attack! Marriage is under attack! There is a war going on!

As we know, the enemy comes to kill, steal, and to destroy. We have to raise a standard! We have to stand up and stand in the gap! Time out for patty cake, cute prayers, this is WAR! We have to stop, drop and pray! Not later, NOW!

There is a spirit of rebellion attacking the marriage union. Marriage does not look like it used to as a result. Husbands are trying to control, instead of lead and love their wives. Wives are trying to lead, instead of submitting and respecting their husbands.

I challenge you to begin praying against the spirit of rebellion in your marriage and other marriages. Ask the Lord to rebuke the enemy, read satan his rights, ask God to dispatch angels, declare healing, declare restoration, declare reconciliation, pray for other marriages, lift your sisters up in prayer as they walk in their roles, pray for their husbands to take and maintain their rightful positions. Pray diligently, pray battle prayers, and speak victory confessions.

To the sisters who are struggling in faith, hurting, and on the verge of giving up....

Faint not! In due season, you will reap a harvest! Hold your head up! We've got your back, but we need you, too.

Rise up, Warrior!

Take up your cross, grab your sword, and prepare to fight! You play a part in the manifestation of those praying for you and the manifestation of your own prayers. The battle is not given to the swift, but to the one that endures.

Do not become weary in well doing. Pick up a Bible and start reading! Download a Bible app. Start learning and memorizing scripture pertaining to your marriage and your situation. Fill your ears with the Word.

It is time out for ratchet TV and the latest reality shows. I'm not against those things if that's what you like to do, but honey your marriage is on the line. It is time to do everything you can and everything you know to get your breakthrough. Turn off the TV and turn on the Word. Turn down the radio and turn up your praise!

Warriors, rise up! Do not lose faith or waver one bit. Stop, drop, and pray!

I DECLARE WAR!!

Wives, grab your sword (Bible). Review the following confession of faith and if you agree, hold your sword with your right hand and read these words out loud:

Father God in the name of Jesus,

Forgive me for my sins, known and unknown. Continue to cleanse me from all unrighteousness. Father, I am standing up for marriage. I am standing up for victory in marriage. I declare, as the Word says, no weapon formed against me shall prosper. Every tongue that rises against me shall be put to shame. Every negative word I have spoken against my marriage and my husband, I uproot it in the name of Jesus. I plead the blood of Jesus where the seed is uprooted.

I plead the blood of Jesus over my marriage. I ask that you put a hedge of protection over my marriage, over my husband, over me, over our home, our family, and our finances. From this day forward I will strive to keep a guard over my lips. From this day forward I will aim to use the power of influence you have given me to encourage and build up my husband. I declare that my husband has taken his rightful position as head of our family. I declare that my husband loves me as Christ loves the church. I declare that my husband does not deal with me harshly and he dwells with me with understanding.

I declare that I respect my husband. I respect the authority that you have given my husband over me and I trust that you have the power to lead me through my husband. Allow my marriage to be an example of what you ordained and designed marriage to me.

Guide my husband, order his steps. Help me to be the suitable helper that he needs. Father, help me to renew my mind so that I can be intentional with my words in my marriage and in all areas of my life. Your word says that whatever I ask if I believe it shall be given unto me. I ask all of these things, Father, and I declare them as already done.

It is your will for marriage to be lasting. It is your will for my husband to walk in his purpose. It is your will for me to walk in my purpose. It is your will that we are blessed so that we can be a blessing. I thank you for your will in every area of my life, in the name of Jesus!

I stand in agreement with other wives who believe you for restoration and reconciliation. I stand in agreement with other wives who are taking on the silent warrior challenge and praying for their husbands.

I thank you for your angels of protection and for giving your angels charge over me and my husband to keep us in all of our ways. I declare that from this day forward, even if we stumble we will not fall because you uphold us with your right hand. Create in me a clean heart, O God, and renew a steadfast spirit within me. Restore to me the joy of your salvation and grant me a willing spirit to sustain me. In the name of Jesus, I pray. Amen!

Listen, do not get in the ring if you are not equipped. This is not a game. As you press, the enemy will press back. You have to be ready. If you are not ready, spend some time in prayer for a little while before you jump in the ring.

Wives, will you join me in the fight for marriage? If you accept the silent warrior challenge, I would like to hear from you. Send me an email, follow me on social media, let's stand with one accord!

Reflection
Do you want to win the battle or do you want to win the war? Are you ready to take the silent warrior challenge?

Victory Verse
"We wrestle not against flesh and blood, but against principalities, against powers, against the rulers of the darkness of this world, against spiritual wickedness in high places." Ephesians 6:12

Prayer
Father God, in the name of Jesus, I want to be a prayer warrior for marriage. I want to take a stand and be a part of raising a standard

Chapter 9

The Power of Love

"Love never fails...."1 Corinthians 13:8

Love Wins...and that is a fact. It was love when God gave us life. It was love that led Jesus to die on the cross. It was love when you married your husband. It was love that led you here.

Love will cover and keep your marriage, if you walk in it. The only way you know that you have unconditional love is when conditions come and you get through them. The Bible says that in marriage there will be trouble (1 Corinthians 7:28). It is in the Word! There is no escaping it; however, how you go through the trouble is what counts.

You have everything you need to be successful in marriage. You have the Word of God, the Bible. You have direct access to God, to pray for direction and guidance. You have access to tools that can be used to invest in your marriage (classes, books, marriage retreats, etc.). You have the love of God. You just have to implement what you have.

MY STORY

My marriage started off rough. We thought we knew what we were doing. We thought that since we prayed and fasted before getting married that we would be okay. One prayer will not keep your marriage intact. Simply knowing God and going to church will not keep your marriage together. It takes a lot of effort to make marriage work. It takes a lot of forgiveness and a lot of love.

I hurt my husband with my mouth. I cursed him with my words. I spoke too much, early in my marriage and had to deal with the repercussions. These are things you can avoid if you employ the wisdom of the Bible within your marriage.

It took me a while to stop trying to impose my ideas and beliefs onto my husband. I had to learn that I cannot make my husband see what I see, think what I think, or feel how I feel. It just does not work that way, at least not regularly. I have made myself frustrated so many times surrounding this. Now, I pray and ask God to show my husband things or help him to understand things. Ask God to get your point across to your understand. Save yourself the headache.

As I said in the Introduction, I am no relationship expert. What I have shared is from personal experience. My experience includes a painful divorce (yes, this is my second marriage). My experience includes marital counseling with the Pastor and with a professional marriage & family counselor.

My experience includes individual counseling with a therapist. My experience includes phone calls and conversations with seasoned wives, those who have been married 10 or more years. My experience includes blood, sweat, and tears; sore knees (from praying), hoarse voice (from praying), and a grumbling stomach (from fasting).

WITHOUT A WORD

The Bible talks about how an unbelieving husband can be won over without a word. Whether your husband is a believer, walking in his purpose, or not, I believe he can be won over. Your conduct and how you walk out your role as wife plays a huge part.

It is time to focus on doing your part and fight on your knees. Fight silently and in the Spirit. Hold your peace and let the Lord fight any battle that comes.

Allow God to deal with your husband and stay out of the way. Walk in the fruits of the spirit. Walk in forgiveness. Walk in love.

Keep yourself in right standing with God and know that He will deal with your husband. If your husband is mistreating you, please know that God sees it and He will not allow your husband to continue to mistreat you. The important part is staying anchored to God and making sure you are doing what you are supposed to do, as a believer.

Remember, it is not about how we feel or what we think. God knew at the altar when you made your vow what was ahead. We did not know, but God did.

Some of these husbands will not make it in without their wives. For this reason, we must take our role as a wife seriously. Your husband's salvation may be on the line. Your husband's purpose and destiny may be on the line.

ACCOUNTABILITY

I encourage you to pray about getting an accountability partner for your marriage. The accountability partner should be a seasoned married couple who can help you and your husband to stay focused and on track.. They should also be willing to pray with you and your husband, offering Godly wisdom and advice to help make your marriage stronger.

My husband was not initially on board with the idea of an accountability partner. The first time I brought it up, he said he would think about it and never got back to me. The next time I brought it up we were at the First Comes Love marriage retreat.

A couple married for 18 years, taught a session on communication. It was a power packed, very informative session. The following day at the retreat when this same couple walked into the meeting room, I heard "accountability partners."

I did not say anything to my husband in that moment. I silently prayed. As the daily sessions were coming to an end, I wrote my husband a short note and passed it to him. The note simply asked him what he thought about this particular couple being our accountability partners. He slightly nodded, giving me the indication that he would consider my idea. Then, the master of ceremony said, "Some of you need to make sure you do not leave this retreat without an accountability partner." I could have shouted and ran around the room! Talk about confirmation!

Needless to say, we discussed the idea during our session break and my husband agreed. I was grateful and knew this meant God was going to do something great in our lives. We spoke with this couple later that day and they agreed to be our accountability partners.

My husband has established a friendship with the husband and I have established a friendship with the wife. We speak with them privately and we have sessions where all four of us are involved. We are already implementing tools they have given us and it is working.

Accountability partners help to keep you accountable. They are there to offer support and encouragement. They are also there to tell you the difficult things or let you know when you are out of order or out of line. There has to be a level of trust built, more so, trust in God for this type of situation to work.

The purpose of the accountability partner relationship is to ensure you are linked with like-minded individuals who want to see your marriage last and want to see you do what God says. There is a double blessing in this kind of partnership. Just as our accountability partners pray for us, we pray for them, too, sincerely. Our accountability partners have become like family

If your husband is where my husband was with this idea in the beginning, do not worry about it. Pray and wait. In the meantime, seek to lock forces with a sister who is stronger than you, more seasoned in marriage than you, and who will help talk you off the ledge when you are ready to jump. Not a gossip buddy. You need an accountability partner! You need the kind of person who does not need intimate details and will pray and intercede for you, anyway. You need the kind of person who will fast with and for you. I am talking about the kind of person who will advise you NOT to speak or do anything contrary to God's Word.

MAKE AN INVESTMENT

You made an investment in your marriage when you purchased this book. (Or someone else made an investment in your marriage, when they purchased this book for you) I specifically prayed for every hand that would touch or hold this book and every marriage that is connected to that hand. I declare that your investment will be multiplied!

It is imperative that you continue to invest in your marriage. Buy and read books. Attend workshops and conferences. Go to a marriage retreat.

My husband and I recently attended our first marriage retreat and it was life changing. We went to the First Comes

Love Marriage Retreat held annually in Arizona. We learned about communication, sex, finances, rebuilding trust, forgiveness, and so much more. We connected with other like-minded couples and we connected with one another.

We came home from the retreat more in love with one another than we had ever been. This may be what you and your husband need. Maybe you need a few days alone, to be together and with God, to connect, or to reconnect. Make the investment!

There is nothing more important to invest in besides your marriage, other than your relationship with God. You made a vow, a lifelong commitment with your husband. That is a long time. Your investment in your marriage will multiply. It will show for itself and it will be worth it.

SHUT YOUR MOUTH

Ladies, love will see you through, if you allow it to. Stand on God's Word. Do not be the blessing blocker or husband hater. This is not a game! This is a matter of life and death, literally.

Satan has been telling lies from the beginning. He wants you to believe that you need to vent and get things off of your chest. He is using this lie in marriages all over the world! Where in the Bible does it say that it is okay to vent?

Shut your mouth, if you are not speaking God's Word over your husband and marriage. Folks do not need to know your business. You do not have to vent. You do not have to get anything off of your chest. All you have to do is pray!

I am not saying that we should not communicate with our husbands. You should be able to have a conversation and talk about things. However, it is best to saturate your words with prayer so that what you say is received. How you say something and when you say it is just as important as what you say. Master the art of silence. Allow God to guide your words and the timing of their delivery.

In fact, you are accountable for every thought you allow to take residence in your mind. When a negative thought about your husband enters your mind, do not allow it to take root. Counter it. Negate it. If you are able to, speak the opposite, something positive, immediately.

We are told to bring every thought captive and make it align with the Word of God (2 Corinthians 10:5). We are to think on whatever is true, noble, right, pure, lovely, and admirable (Philippians 4:8). If our hearts are focused on thinking on the right things, as instructed by the Word, our words will line up as well because out of the abundance of the heart, the mouth speaks (Matthew 12:34).

The Bible says that peacemakers are blessed (Matthew 5:9). I do not know about you but I want to be blessed in Let's shut our mouths and get on our knees!

Reflection
Do you believe in the power of love? Do you believe that love conquers all? Are you allowing love to cover your husband and all areas of your marriage?

Prayer
Father God, in the name of Jesus, thank you for the gift of love and the power of love. Thank you for loving me. Show me how to walk in love towards my husband. Show me how to allow love to cover and conquer with my marriage. Teach

me how to love my husband unconditionally and teach my husband how to love me unconditionally. Amen.

Confession

I walk in love towards my husband and within my marriage. I allow love to cover and conquer all.

Chapter 10

The Power of Confessions

"Death and life are in the power of the tongue: and they that love it shall eat the fruit thereof." Proverbs 18:21

The Bible says you will be ensnared by the words of your mouth (Proverbs 6:2). Ensnared means trapped or entangled. If I am going to be trapped by my words, I want to make sure my words are trapping me into something wonderful and great. How about you?

The world uses positive affirmations or positive statements as a tool to inspire and encourage self. Affirmations are known to help overcome negative thoughts. The method is the more you speak the affirmations, you begin to trick your brain. What you once did not believe you start to believe. The goal is to change negative thinking into positive thinking so that a negative life becomes a positive life.

Declaring positive affirmations is actually in line with biblical principles and this is one reason it is so effective. Believers call our affirmations a confession of faith. A confession of faith is an acknowledgement of your belief. It is a statement that declares the very thing you believe and hope for. A confession of faith is a declarative statement that is lined up with the word of God.

God's Word cannot return to Him void. When we declare the Word of God affirmatively and in faith, we are speaking with authority. We are planting seeds into the atmosphere. A confession is intended to help strengthen your faith and help manifest what you hope for, as long as it is in God's will.

The first time I wrote a confession it was during a time when my faith was challenged. I was uncertain about who I was in Christ. I was uncertain about the promises of God that I had heard about. I had not had a real experience with God, yet, and I struggled to believe some things that were in His Word.

I went through my Bible and located scriptures about my identity in Christ. I located scriptures about simple things that I had a hard time believing at that time. I took those scriptures and turned them into positive affirmations that I could declare daily. As I began to confess what I had written, my life began to change. The same thing happened within my marriage.

First, I was *confessing* the things I did not want. I was confessing the negative things about my husband and my marriage. The more I confessed what I did not want and what was negative, the more I received that very thing.

As I began to shift and focus on God's word and promises, my thinking changed. Then, my words changed. My confessions are now confident declarations of what is and what is to come.

I encourage you to write your own confessions, if you have not already. Get in the habit of declaring God's word over your marriage, your husband, yourself, your children, your finances, etc. Call those things that are not, as though they were, until they are. Amen?

I will share my first confession of faith with you, in hopes that it will encourage those who are struggling in their faith. I also hope that it will strengthen those who know the Word to be true and simply need a reminder of the basics. I will also share a few confessions that you can read daily regarding your marriage and your journey to becoming a silent warrior. Each confession I am sharing I have used in my own life.

The Bible tells us to call those things that are not as though they were. That's what confessions do. As you confess, you create. Words have creative power, remember? When you add the force of specifically confessing the Word of God you are guaranteed to see results.

It is time for you to create what is missing or lacking in your marriage and your husband. If nothing is missing or lacking at this time, great! I still encourage you to create a confession of faith for things you want to see in your marriage and your husband.

If you need to see more love in your life, confess it. If you need to see healing in your life, confess it. Look up every scripture pertaining to anything you need and put together a confession to help change your life. If you do this in addition to being a silent warrior, you are GUARANTEED to see life changing results in your marriage and in your life!

There is an awesome daily confession that I have participated in through an organization called Wife Talk, Inc. The group confession takes place Monday thru Friday at 5:30 am EST. It is broadcast on Periscope, under WifeTalkO7. Treshelle Williams, the Founder of Wife Talk, Inc. leads the confession. She reads the confession and you repeat it. If confessing the word is new to you or if you just need or want additional support, especially in the company of other wives who are believers, check it out.

Remember, life and death are in the power of the tongue. The Word also tells us that we will be ensnared by the words of our mouth and we shall have what we say. What are you saying?

The following is a list of confessions included at the back of this book, in the Resources section.
1. My first confession of faith (make it your own)
2. *You Talk Too Much* confession of faith (The confession from each chapter, compiled into one for you to read daily)
3. A confession of faith about my husband
4. A confession of faith about me
5. A confession of faith about marriage and sex

Feel free to copy, rewrite, and tailor the confessions to suit your needs and the needs within your marriage. Some of the confessions repeat the same scriptures and/or principles. The intent is for you to select the confession or confessions that work best for you. You do not have to read all of them. You do not have to use any of them. They are included to simply encourage you to get in the routine of creating confessions of faith and declaring the Word of God in your life and in your marriage, regularly. Enjoy!

Reflection
What are you intentionally putting into the atmosphere with your mouth? Are you confessing the Word of God?

Victory Verse
"Truly, I say to you, whoever says to this mountain, 'Be taken up and thrown into the sea,' and does not doubt in his heart, but believes that what he says will come to pass, it will be done for him." Mark 11:23

Prayer
Father God, in the name of Jesus, your word cannot return to you void. Your Word says that whatever I ask, according to Your will, if I believe and do not doubt in my heart, you will give me what I ask. I ask for your will in my marriage. I ask for renewed love between my husband and me. I ask for a strong, solid, loving, and lasting marriage. Thank you for revealing to me the power of confessing your word. I commit to declaring your Word in my marriage and in my husband. Amen.

Confession
I will confess the Word of God in faith and confidence. I will declare God's Word over my marriage, my husband, myself, my family, my finances, and my life. The love is renewed between my husband and me. My marriage is strong, solid, loving and lasting.

The Task

Author Unknown

Once upon a time a beautiful girl got tired of her marriage and wanted to kill her spouse. One morning she ran to her mother and said to her, "Mother, I am tired of my husband. I can no longer tolerate his nonsense. I want to kill him but I am afraid the authorities might hold me responsible, can you please help me, mother?"

The mother replied, "Yes, my daughter, I can help you. But there's a little task attached."

The daughter asked, "What task? I am willing and ready to do anything, in order to get him out of my way."

"Okay," said the mother. "Here is the task:

1. You will be forced to make peace with him, so that no one will suspect you when he is eventually dead.

2. You will have to beautify yourself in other to look young and attractive to him.

3. You have to take good care of him and be very nice and appreciative of him.

4. You have to be patient, loving and less jealous. Be just, show respect, pray, be a good helper, and listen to him so that you will never be suspected.

Can you do all of that?" the mother asked.

"Yes, I can," the daughter replied.

"Okay," said the mother.

"Now, take this powder and pour a bit in his meal every day. It will slowly kill him," said the mother.

After 30 days the daughter came back to her mother and said, "Mother, I have no intentions of killing my husband anymore. As of now, I have grown to love him because he has completely changed. He is now a very sweet husband, more than I ever imagined. What can I do to stop the poison you gave me, from killing him? Please, help me mother," she pleaded in a sorrowful tone.

The mother answered, "Do not worry, my daughter. What I gave you was just a rice dust. It will never kill him. In reality, you were the poison that was slowly killing your husband with heat and dispassion. You see, when you started loving and cherishing him, and doing your part, you saw him change. Men are not really wicked. Rather, are weak at heart."

Women, if you can only show love, care, and commitment to your husband, I assure you he will be change and be the man you married and hoped for.

Resources and Recommendations

My First Confession of Faith

I am a child of God, an heir of God, joint-heir with Christ.
I believe in my heart that Jesus Christ is the Son of God.
I believe He was raised from the dead for my justification.
I confess Jesus as my Lord and Savior. Jesus is my Lord.
He is dominating my life. He is guiding me. He is leading me.

The Lord is my Shepherd I do not want. I do not want for ability. I do not want for money. I do not want for anything.
I abide in Him. I live in Him. His word abides in me.
I am a new creature in Christ. I am God's workmanship created in Christ. God made me worthy to stand in His presence as though I've never committed sin.

I am the righteousness of God in Christ.
My standing with God is secure. My prayers avail much.
Because I am in Christ Jesus right now there is no sense of condemnation about me. I have received abundance of grace and the gift of righteousness.

By His stripes I was healed. Healing belongs to me because I am in Christ. The law of life in Christ Jesus has set me free from the law of sin and death. Because I am Christ the greater one lives in me. He is greater than the devil. He is greater than disease. He is greater than circumstances. He is greater than fear and doubt.

I am more than a conqueror. Through Christ my Lord, I can do all things. He strengthens me. I cannot be conquered. I cannot be defeated.

All of my needs are supplied. No weapon formed against me shall prosper. Every tongue that rises against me shall be condemned. My ways are pleasing to God; therefore God has caused my enemies to be at peace with me. He has made my enemies my footstool. God has granted that the enemies who rise against me are defeated before me. For they come in one direction but flee from me in seven

I am blessed. I am anointed. I am guarded. I am valuable. There is a hedge of protection over me & all those whom I come into contact with. The favor of God is upon me. I walk in favor. I am covered in the full armor of God. I wear salvation as my helmet, with the belt of truth buckled around my waist. I wear the breastplate of righteousness.

My feet are fitted with the readiness that comes from the gospel of peace. Faith is my shield and I carry the sword of the spirit. I walk in the fruits of the spirit.

I am blessed in the city and the country. The fruit of my womb is blessed. God has blessed all that he gave me. He has granted me abundant prosperity. I am blessed coming and going. I am the head and not the tail. Everything I need, I already have. And everything I need to know I already know.

Right where I am, God is. I am exactly where I need to be. My steps are divinely and strategically ordered. I can make plans but the Lord determines how they come together.
If I stumble, I will not fall, for God's right hand keeps me and redirects me. If I need it, I have it. If it's no good for me, God will keep me from it.

I walk in wisdom and my spiritual gifts are in full operation. God has given His angels charge over me to keep me in all of my ways. I have the power to tread over serpents and scorpions and all the power of the enemy. Nothing by any means shall hurt or harm me.

Jesus came that I may have life and life more abundantly.
I am walking in abundance. I walk by faith and not by sight.
I operate in a meek and quiet spirit, which is pleasing to God.
I am a cheerful giver, which the Lord loves.
Because I am a giver, God has caused others to give to me in abundance. The blessing is all over me. With my hands I bless. With my mouth I bless. Everything that my hands touch is blessed and has to prosper.

I open my lips to speak what is right; my mouth speaks what is true. For my lips detest wickedness, all the words of my mouth are just. None of them are crooked or perverse.
I honor God with my body which is my reasonable service.
My body is the temple of the Holy Spirit. My body is healthy and in good health and it prospers even as my soul prospers.
I speak strength and energy into my body. My mind is alert, no longer conformed to this world but renewed by the word of God.

If God is for me who can be against me? I am strong in the Lord. I mind my own business. I am a peacemaker. I am focused. I am determined. I am ambitious. I finish what I start. I keep my word. I manage my time well. I do not take on more than I should or more than I am supposed to. I am a confident woman of faith. My gifts have made room for me. I am walking in the blessing. I am living my dreams and walking in my purpose. I am debt free. I manage money well. God will keep me in perfect peace because my mind is stayed on him.

You Talk Too Much
Confession of Faith

(The confession from each chapter, compiled into one for you to read daily)

I open my lips to speak what is right. My mouth speaks what is true. My lips detest wickedness. All the words of my mouth are just; none of them are crooked or perverse.

I am a peacemaker and I am blessed. The words of my mouth and the mediation of my heart are acceptable in God's sight. I rejoice in hope, I am patient in tribulation, and I am constant in prayer.

I am a wife of noble character. My husband's heart safely trusts in me. I am a help to my husband and a blessing in his life. With me by his side, my husband is a mighty man of valor and everything his hands touch is blessed.

I pray for my husband daily. I am attentive to the Holy Spirit and always know what to pray for concerning my husband. I am confident that God hears my prayers and because I am confident that He hears me, I know that He has answered me.

I respect my husband. I show proper respect to him when we are together and when we are apart. My conduct and behavior is pleasing to God and because of my obedience I am blessed.

I love my husband. I desire my husband and my husband desires me. My bosom satisfies my husband all of the days of his life His heart is turned towards me and my heart is turned towards him.

I am intentional with my mouth and my words. I bless others when I speak. I encourage others when I speak. I give hope when I speak and I speak in love.
I walk in love towards my husband and within my marriage. I allow love to cover and conquer all.

I will confess the Word of God in faith and confidence. I will declare God's Word over my marriage, my husband, myself, my family, my finances, and my life. The love is renewed between my husband and me. My marriage is strong, solid, loving and lasting.

Confession of Faith (husband)

My husband loves me, as Christ loves the church.
He loves me honestly, genuinely, and wholeheartedly.
He respects me, he admires me, and he truly cares for me.
He thinks about me when we are apart and he cherishes the time we spend together.

His heart is turned towards me.
He is faithful, honest, and loyal to me.
He is a better man because of me.
He is my husband and he is blessed.
Because he found me, he found a good thing and receives favor from the Lord.
My husband is gainfully employed, financially secure, responsible, hardworking, and dedicated.
He is the sole provider for our family.
He is prayerful and obedient to God.
He prays for me and over me.
We communicate effectively and we work together as a team.
We enjoy time together immensely.
My husband feels safe with me. His heart safely trusts in me.
He is proud to call me his woman, his leading lady, his wife.
We make love and it's magical, all of the time.
We are in tune with one another, we truly understand one another and we're deeply connected.

Our marriage is precious. It is honorable in the eyes of God. It is esteemed worthy. Our marriage is blessed.

We are debt free. We are financial responsible. We are faithful stewards over our finances, our children, and all that is within our care and ownership.

My husband calls me blessed. I submit to my husband as unto the Lord. We submit one to another. We take care of our own together and we take care of each other.

Confession of Faith (me)

I am a wife of noble character. My husband's heart safely trusts in me. I am a confident woman of faith.
I was created in the image and likeness of God. I was made with a purpose, for a duty, and an assignment. I am beautiful. I am important. I am necessary. I am an extraordinary woman of God.

I am strong in the Lord in the power of his might. I am the righteousness of God in Christ. I walk in dominion, power, favor, and righteousness. I am already perfect (whole, complete, lacking nothing) as my Father in heaven is perfect (whole, complete, lacking nothing). I am victorious, triumphant, overcoming, and winning in every area of my life. I have overcome by the blood of the Lamb and the word of my testimony. I abide under the shadow of the almighty, and I am protected. Because I make the Kingdom of God and its righteousness my top priority all that I require, all that I need, is added to me in ever increasing amounts according to God's will. In the name of Jesus!!

God has given me the power to get wealth. I lack and want for nothing. I declare that all of my needs are supplied and my cup runs over and overflows. Jesus came that I may have life and life more abundantly. I am walking in abundance!!

I bring the tithes and offerings to the storehouse and therefore God has rebuked the devourer for my sake. God has

opened up the windows of heaven and poured out blessings so big that I don't even have room enough to receive!
I am a giver and God has caused men to give unto me, good measured, pressed down, shaken together and running over. I have more than enough. I am living in abundance. I am the lender and not the borrower. I am totally and completely debt free and I owe no man anything except love. Goodness and mercy follows me all the days of my life and I will dwell in the house of the Lord forever.

God speaks to me and I do what He tells me to do. I clearly know His promptings in my heart. When He speaks I know it's Him and I obey Him, the voice of a stranger I will never follow. My steps are strategically and divinely ordered in the name of Jesus. God has called me to lead nations; He knows the thoughts and plans He has for me. They are thoughts of good and not evil, plans to give me a hope and a future with an expected end. I walk in the fruits of the spirit keeping the kingdom of God and all its righteousness my top priority. I walk in love, joy, peace, patience, kindness, goodness, faithfulness, gentleness and self-control.

I was created in the image and likeness of God. I was made with a purpose, for a duty, and an assignment. I am beautiful. I am important. I am necessary. I am a confident woman of God. I am an extraordinary woman of God.

Confession of Faith (Marriage & Sex)

In the name of Jesus, I declare I am a virtuous woman of God and the perfect and only wife for my husband. I declare my husband is the perfect and only husband for me and he is a mighty man of valor.

I am the crown he cherishes and a gift to his life. He only has eyes for me and I only have eyes for him. Divorce and legal separation are not an option. We walk together in love, on one accord and in serving God. Our marriage is successful because it's anointed by God.

My husband is the spiritual leader of our household and has a heart after God. My husband has taken his rightful position as the head and heart is open to hear from God. His heart is tender toward God's Word.

My husband follows the prompting and leading of the Holy Spirit. His steps are strategically and divinely ordered. I declare and decree that my husband seeks first the kingdom of God and His righteousness and he is walking in God's statutes. My husband is the sole provider for our family and household. He is a faithful steward over our finances and is wise is money management.

My husband is filled with the Holy Spirit. He is anointed and he believes in the Word of God. My husband does not trust how he feels, what he hears or sees, because his faith is in the Word of God.

He walks by faith and not by sight. The Word of God is the final authority in our lives and in our marriage.

My husband spends much time in prayer, much time in God's Word and he is walking in integrity, honesty and has morals based on the Word of God. He has control over his thought life and his emotions. He guards his lips and his tongue. He opens his mouth to speak what is true and his lips detest wickedness. He is kept in perfect peace because his mind is stayed on Jesus.

I declare that my husband is the father that he is called to be to his children. He raises them in the wisdom of God. He is a strong, positive, Godly influence and example. My husband has an anointing to pray for his family and keeps us covered daily.

I plead the blood of Jesus over my husband and over our marriage. No weapon formed against us, or our marriage, can prosper. My husband values what I say; my opinions and suggestions are weighty to him and his decision-making process because like the Holy Spirit I serve as a help to my husband and I serve as a wise counselor.

My husband grants me favor. He thinks highly of me. He respects me and loves me as Christ loves the church. He does not deal with me harshly but treats me as the weaker vessel in love, with respect, with understanding, and with grace. He loves me as Christ loves the church and he gave up his life for me as Christ gave up His life for the church.

My husband covers me with love. He protects me gracefully. He ensures my needs are met, I don't go without, and I am well care of.

I bind, abort, destroy and cancel every plan and assignment the devil would bring against my husband and our marriage. I plead the blood of Jesus over my husband wherever he goes. God has given angels charge over him to keep him in all of his ways.

When lies flood my mind regarding the status of our marriage or when it doesn't feel like a honeymoon, I declare we will strive to recognize the lies & kill them at their root. May we recognize the ungodliness hiding in our own will, expectations and how we express our emotions.

I declare that I will never give up on our marriage. My husband and I are in agreement; we won't give up! I declare that I will always pray for my marriage and my husband.

Satan, the Lord rebukes you! I plead the blood of Jesus against every adulterous spirit, lust of the world, lust of the flesh, flirting spirit, spirit of pornography, the spirit of antichrist, spirit of perversion, rebellious spirits, the lust of the eyes and the love of money. I abort and cancel any backbiting spirits and any curses or arguments against me, my husband, and our marriage. They are destroyed in Jesus' name!

I bind, abort and destroy every trick and trap of the devil off our lives. I loose peace, joy, love, contentment, unity, appreciation for one another, forgiveness, prosperity, sober minds, wisdom, health and long life upon us and our children.

I decree that my husband makes right and wise decisions, because he seeks God first. I declare the blessing of prosperity, blessings of God's favor is upon my husband's life and the blessing of health in his physical body.

We have the mind of Christ; we think and act like Jesus even in trials and stressful situations. We believe, stand on and act upon the Word. We are led by the Holy Spirit, not by our feelings or emotions or other peoples' opinions. My husband is the head and not the tail, above only and not beneath, the lender and not the borrower.

I declare that every time my husband and I are intimate it is sweet, extremely satisfying, and enjoyable. Our sex life is on fire, without pain or discomfort, and pleasures us both. I declare that my body functions the way it is supposed to and so does my husband's body. We become closer together after each sexual encounter.

My husband is faithful and loyal. His heart is turned towards me. My bosom satisfies him. He is attracted to me. He desires me. He loves my scent and is drawn to me.

I am faithful and loyal to my husband. My heart is turned towards him. He satisfies me I am attracted to him. I desire him. I am drawn to him.

My husband safely trusts in me and he confides in me. I do not betray his confidence and trust. I am a safe place for my husband.

We walk in love daily, respecting one another and esteeming the other higher than ourselves. We submit one to the other. We love, respect and honor God. We see each other as God sees us. We allow God's transforming Word to transform our motives, emotions and will. I declare we walk in forgiveness and walk in the fruit of the Spirit.

I declare an increased anointing upon my husband to win sinner's hearts for the kingdom of God. I declare that our steps are ordered by the Lord and He causes us to know the way in which we are to walk. We surrender ourselves and our marriage to God and invite God to have His way in our life.

The Lord teaches me how to show my husband respect and how to support and encourage him daily. Thank You, Lord, for coaching and guiding me relentlessly to be a wife who respects her own husband in thought, word and deed.

My husband consults God about everything before doing anything, like King David did. I decree my husband is in God's will at all times. In Jesus name, Amen

The Scripture Says...

Proverbs 10:19 - In the multitude of words there wanteth not sin: but he that refraineth his lips [is] wise.

Proverbs 17:27 - He that hath knowledge spareth his words: [and] a man of understanding is of an excellent spirit.

Proverbs 17:28 - Even a fool, when he holdeth his peace, is counted wise: [and] he that shutteth his lips [is esteemed] a man of understanding.

Proverbs 18:2 - A fool hath no delight in understanding, but that his heart may discover itself.

Proverbs 18:21 - Death and life [are] in the power of the tongue: and they that love it shall eat the fruit thereof.

Proverbs 29:20 - Seest thou a man [that is] hasty in his words? [there is] more hope of a fool than of him.

Proverbs 21:23 - Whoso keepeth his mouth and his tongue keepeth his soul from troubles.

Proverbs 13:3 - He that keepeth his mouth keepeth his life: [but] he that openeth wide his lips shall have destruction.

Proverbs 14:23 - In all labour there is profit: but the talk of the lips [tendeth] only to penury.

Proverbs 30:32 - If thou hast done foolishly in lifting up thyself, or if thou hast thought evil, [lay] thine hand upon thy mouth.

Proverbs 15:1 - A soft answer turneth away wrath: but grievous words stir up anger.

Proverbs 15:28 - The heart of the righteous studieth to answer: but the mouth of the wicked poureth out evil things.

Proverbs 12:18 - There is that speaketh like the piercings of a sword: but the tongue of the wise [is] health.

Proverbs 15:4 - A wholesome tongue [is] a tree of life: but perverseness therein [is] a breach in the spirit.

Psalms 118:5 - I called upon the LORD in distress: the LORD answered me, [and set me] in a large place.

Psalms 141:3 - Set a watch, O LORD, before my mouth; keep the door of my lips.

Psalms 19:14 - Let the words of my mouth, and the meditation of my heart, be acceptable in thy sight, O LORD, my strength, and my redeemer.

James 1:19 - Wherefore, my beloved brethren, let every man be swift to hear, slow to speak, slow to wrath:

James 1:26 - If any man among you seem to be religious, and bridleth not his tongue, but deceiveth his own heart, this man's religion [is] vain.

James 3:6 - And the tongue [is] a fire, a world of iniquity: so is the tongue among our members, that it defileth the whole body, and setteth on fire the course of nature; and it is set on fire of hell.

James 3:8 - But the tongue can no man tame; [it is] an unruly evil, full of deadly poison.

Ecclesiastes 5:2 - Be not rash with thy mouth, and let not thine heart be hasty to utter [any] thing before God: for God [is] in heaven, and thou upon earth: therefore let thy words be few.

Ecclesiastes 5:7 - For in the multitude of dreams and many words [there are] also [divers] vanities: but fear thou God.

Ecclesiastes 9:17 - The words of wise [men are] heard in quiet more than the cry of him that ruleth among fools.

Matthew 12:36 - But I say unto you, That every idle word that men shall speak, they shall give account thereof in the day of judgment.

2 Timothy 2:16 - But shun profane [and] vain babblings: for they will increase unto more ungodliness.

Amos 5:13 - Therefore the prudent shall keep silence in that time; for it [is] an evil time.

1 Peter 3:10 - For he that will love life, and see good days, let him refrain his tongue from evil, and his lips that they speak no guile:

Ephesians 4:29 - Let no corrupt communication proceed out of your mouth, but that which is good to the use of edifying, that it may minister grace unto the hearers.

Philippians 2:14 - Do all things without murmurings and disputings:

Other Books by the Author

Live Your Dream Now is a blueprint to show you how to make your dream come true. In this captivating testimony, Tanya DeFreitas shares her journey of taking a dream she held since childhood and the process she took to make her dream a reality. What is inside of you waiting to be birthed? This book provides five steps to help you manifest YOUR dream.

AVAILABLE NOW
On Amazon.com, iBooks, Barnes & Noble, and Kobo!

Order your copy today!

Coming Soon... from the Author

If you enjoyed reading **You Talk Too Much: A Wife's Guide to Becoming a Silent Warrior**, then you will absolutely love and appreciate the **You Talk Too Much Journal Workbook**!

As you take the 30-day Silent Warrior Challenge, the journal workbook will help guide you into a developing a deeper, stronger prayer life. The journal workbook includes reflection questions and exercises to help you to connect or reconnect with your husband. This tool will lead you on an exploratory journey that will help transform your marriage.

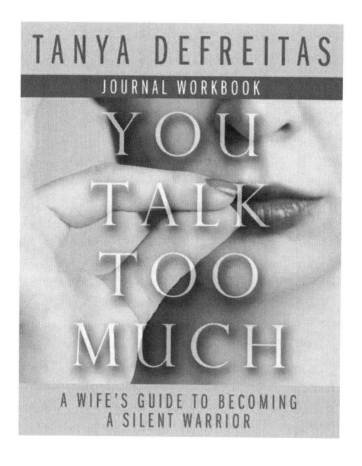

Book Recommendations

The Power of a Praying Wife by Stormie Omartian

Love & Respect by Dr. Emerson Eggerichs

The 5 Love Languages by Gary Chapman

Kingdom Marriage by Tony Evans

Love Dare by Alex Kendrick

Boundaries in Marriage by Henry Cloud

Self-Published Books by Friends

A Wife's Daily Prayer Confession: 31 Days of Powerful Life Changing Confessions by Treshelle Williams

From Pieces to Peace: Damaged Goods by Robin Major-Oliphant

Meek Season: Divorce & Dating by Tamika Smith

Meek Season 2: Discovery & Destiny by Tamika Smith

Who Am I? A Survivor & Not my Past by TK Clemons

Imagine That! 31 Days of Purpose-Filled Analogies

'Imagine That!' is a collection of analogies that encourages thought provoking solutions. As you read through the guided stories, clarity and understanding begin to unfold. Sherry has applied analogies to everyday life situations that many of us have experienced. Your perception and visualization will come alive as you engage in this book.

Available on Amazon.com

The Cure for Adolescence: Applying Biblical Principles to Your Daily Life

The tween, teen and young adult years are awkward for both the parent and the child. Hormonal issues, societal pressures, moral dilemmas, and frontal lobe brain development make navigating life for the adolescent a challenge. If only there were a "cure" for such troubles, life would be simpler. This devotional has been designed to transform the lives of the reader and assist in developing a habit of spending time with God. It is geared towards today's adolescents and poses "the cure" to daily life struggles. It is best received when guided by a parent or with a study group.

Available on Amazon.com

Book Club Discussion Starters

- Do you think you talk too much?

- What boundaries do you think should be put in place when we talk to our friends about our marriage?

- Can you recall a time when you paused and prayed before responding to your husband?

- Which chapter resonated with you the most?

- How are you operating in your role as a suitable helper?

- Do you regularly pray for your husband?

- What does respect mean to you?

- What is your husband's love language?

- Did you have a confession of faith before reading this book?

- What are 3 takeaways to will help you in marriage?

- Are you taking the Silent Warrior challenge? Why or why not?

First Comes Love Marriage Retreat

Are you looking to reconnect with your husband?

Would you like to meet other like-minded Christian couples whose goal is to make their marriage last?

Check out the First Comes Love Marriage Retreat.

http://firstcomeslovemarriageretreat.com

Wife Talk, Inc.

Are you seeking to connect with other married and engaged women?

Experience Wife Talk; a place where we inspire, encourage, and uplift each other. This is a safe, friendly, and support-enriched environment for wives at all stages of wife-hood. Wife Talk is a faith based organization, for wives and women who are engaged to be married ONLY!

Check us out on Facebook!

Wife Talk Safe House

A program of Wife Talk, Inc., Safe Wife was created to address the issue of abuse of married and engaged women. If you need someone to speak with, who will also pray with and for you, contact Safe Wife.

www.safewife.org

If you or someone you know is being abused, please contact:

The National Domestic Violence Hotline

1-800-799-7233
TTY 1-800-787-3224

Get help without saying a word. Online chat is also available 24/7/365

www.thehotline.org

Acknowledgements

To my husband, Rafael P. DeFreitas, Jr., thank you for your unconditional love, commitment, and loyalty to me and our marriage. We have weathered a few storms, yet we always came out dry. You are my knight in shining armor! You are an amazing husband, a dynamic provider, and a great father. Thank you for the inspiration to write this book and for the input and feedback that you provided. I love you and I am forever grateful that God saw fit for you to find me. May you receive favor all the days of your life!
Thank you to my mother, Carla Harvey, for your continued support, love, and prayers.

Thank you to my mother-in-love, Dr. Olivia Jones Mack, for your fervent prayers and Godly wisdom. You never gave up on us and continued to pray even when we seemed to have loss all hope.

Thank you to my father-in-love, Rafael P. DeFreitas, Sr., for your encouragement, love, wisdom, and support.

Thank you, Pastor Clyde Stewart and First Lady Florence Stewart. Pastor, your time, wisdom, encouragement, and prayers helped my marriage to overcome. First Lady, thank you for listening and being so loving and understanding. I appreciate and respect you both dearly.

Thank you, Eddie & Kristina Coleman for being the couple who holds my husband and me accountable to God's way and God's Word in marriage. I cherish the friendship we have developed with you.

Thank you, Mrs. Sherry Pitts, for getting in the trenches with me, praying, fasting, and confessing the Word over my marriage. Thank you for your transparency and for always being positive no matter how bad I made it seem.

Thank you, Mrs. Paula Valle Castanon. You talked me off of the ledge when I was seriously about to jump. Your loving and graceful words restored my faith and hope in God and my marriage.

Thank you, Chavon & LaKiesha Townsel for being a beacon of hope to married couples. Your love for one another and your passion for the First Comes Love Marriage retreat are truly appreciated.

Thank you to the ladies of Wife Talk San Bernardino Chapter. Special shout out to Lakeisha Walker-Spencer, Eumika Augustine Rivers, Shanaita Caldwell, Charletta Yancy-Williams, Tara Mitchell, and Verna Duckworth. Our conversations gave me hope. Your transparency and testimonies inspired and encouraged me. Thank you for your prayers and support.

Thank you to the ladies of Wife Talk South Bay Chapter. Special shout out to Coco Dixon, Tenisha Collins, and Yolanda Johnson. Coco you were there during a few of my "midnight hours" and offered encouragement and support that helped me get to my morning. Tenisha, the confession of faith you shared with me was life changing. Yolanda, my leadership training buddy, thank you being who you are and for being a sister to me. Thank you all for your sisterhood and for being an advocate for #StrongMarriage!

Thank you to my sisters & closest girlfriends, Trina Brown, Kisha Herbert, Fotima Hall, Charmaine Shingleton, & Tiana Burton. I know I gave you each an earful from time to time. Thank you for listening and being there for me. Thank you for not holding an ugly picture of my husband in your minds as a result of me talking too much. Thank you for being a listening ear even during the times that I was out of order. I know better now. I cherish our sisterhood and I love each of you to life!

Thank you Treshelle Williams and Wife Talk, Inc. Wife Talk is the first group for wives that I was a part of. The sisterhood is real. The focus on doing marriage God's way is strong. Treshelle, your vision was and is amazing. You are amazing. Thank you for doing what God told you to do. Thank you for your leadership. Thank you for the conversations we have had about marriage. You have taught me more than I can express. I admire you and I respect you, dearly.

Thank you, Wife Code, The Real Wives, and Wifey – A Support Group. The wifely sisterhood within these groups has offered me encouragement and lots of laughter!

Made in the USA
Middletown, DE
05 February 2019